Birds of Washington

Field Guide

by Stan Tekiela

ADVENTURE PUBLICATIONS, INC.
CAMBRIDGE, MINNESOTA

TO MY WIFE KATHERINE AND DAUGHTER ABIGAIL WITH ALL MY LOVE

ACKNOWLEDGMENTS:

Special thanks to Anthony Hertzel for the range maps and to Sandy Livoti for her exceptional eye to detail.

Book design and illustrations by Jonathan Norberg

Photo credits by photographer and page number:

Cover photo: Bullock's Oriole by Brian E. Small
Brian Collins: 170 **Cornell Laboratory of Ornithology**: 66 (female), 70 **Dembinsky Photo Associates**: 250 (both) **Dudley Edmondson**: 10, 12, 16, 18, 20 (soaring), 46 (soaring), 48 (breeding), 50 (all), 74, 78, 84 (female), 90 (both), 106, 108, 120 (in flight), 122, 126 (both), 128 (yellow-shafted male), 132, 156 (soaring light morph), 158 (both), 160 (perching light morph), 168, 178 (chick-feeding adult, juvenile), 198 (male), 204, 210 (male), 218 (both), 220, 228, 268 (breeding), 270 (breeding), 276 (breeding), 286 (male, winter male), 288, 292 (male), 302 **Don Enger**: 44 (rushing, weed dance) **Kevin T. Karlson**: 36, 136 (both), 140 (female), 272 (breeding), 274 (winter) **Bruce Leventhal**: 282 **Bill Marchel**: 2, 24 (male), 66 (female), 72, 138, 148, 152, 172 (female), 198 (female), 234, 244, 246, 260, 266, 280 **Maslowski Wildlife Productions**: 6 (male), 30 (male), 54, 56 (female), 64, 82, 100, 104, 112, 166, 180, 182, 184, 192, 240 (male), 256 (male), 264, 294, 298, 304 **Steve Mortensen**: 8, 24 (female), 32 (both), 40 (both), 46 (perching), 52, 60, 92, 146, 162, 214, 242, 286 (female), 300 (both) **Warren Nelson**: 128 (yellow-shafted female), 292 (female) **John Pennoyer**: 42, 76, 116, 248, 258 (male) **Brian E. Small**: 6 (female), 26, 28 (both), 30 (female), 34, 44 (breeding), 48 (winter), 56 (male), 58 (both), 62, 68, 84 (Oregon female, gray-headed), 86 (female), 88, 94, 98 (winter), 102, 110 (winter), 114, 128 (red-shafted male and female), 134, 140 (male), 142, 150 (both), 154, 174 (perching), 178 (breeding), 188, 194 (Oregon male), 200, 202, 206 (gray morph), 208, 212 (both), 216, 222, 236 (both), 238 (both), 240 (female), 252, 254, 256 (female), 258 (yellow male), 262, 268 (winter), 270 (winter, juvenile), 272 (winter), 274 (breeding, in flight), 276 (winter), 278 (all), 284 (female), 290, 296 (all) **Stan Tekiela**: 4 (both), 14, 22 (both), 38, 80, 96 (both), 98 (breeding), 106 (1 year old), 110 (breeding), 118, 120 (perching), 124, 130, 144, 164, 172 (male), 176, 186, 190, 194 (male), 196, 210 (female), 218 (juvenile), 226, 230, 232, 268 (in flight), 284 (male) **Brian K. Wheeler**: 20 (perching), 156 (perching light and dark morphs, soaring dark morph, intermediate morph), 160 (perching dark morph, soaring light and dark morphs), 174 (soaring, juvenile), 224 (all) **Jim Zipp**: 206 (brown morph)

To the best of the publisher's knowledge, all photos were of live birds.

Second Printing
Copyright 2001 by Stan Tekiela
Published by Adventure Publications, Inc.
820 Cleveland St. S, Cambridge, MN 55008
1-800-678-7006
All rights reserved
Printed in China

TABLE OF CONTENTS
Introduction

WHY WATCH BIRDS IN WASHINGTON?

Millions of people have discovered bird feeding. It's a simple and enjoyable way to bring the beauty of birds closer to your home. Watching birds at your feeder often leads to a lifetime pursuit of bird identification. The *Birds of Washington Field Guide* is for those who want to identify common birds of Washington.

There are over 800 species of birds found in North America. In Washington alone there have been over 440 different kinds of birds recorded throughout the years. These bird sightings were diligently recorded by hundreds of bird watchers and became part of the official state record. From these valuable records, I've chosen 130 of the most common birds of Washington to include in this field guide.

Bird watching, often called birding, is the largest spectator sport in America. Its outstanding popularity in Washington is due, in part, to an unusually rich and abundant birdlife. Why are there so many birds? One reason is open space. Washington is over 70,000 square miles (182,200 sq. km), making it the nineteenth largest state. Despite its size, only about 6 million people call Washington home. On average, that's only 86 people per square mile (33 per sq. km). Most of these people are located along the Pacific. Over half of the population lives around Puget Sound. This concentration of people leaves plenty of room for birds.

Water, both saltwater and fresh, plays a big part in Washington's bird populations as well. Washington has more than 157 miles (253 km) of coastline, which is home to many ocean-loving birds such as the Double-crested Cormorant and California Gull. In addition to the Pacific coast, Washington has many freshwater and saltwater marshes, not to mention several major rivers, most of which drain into the ocean. All of this water attracts millions of birds such as the American Wigeon and Blue-winged Teal.

Open space and water are not the only reasons there is such an abundance of birds. It's also the diversity of habitat. Washington can be broken into four distinct habitats–Pacific Border, Sierra-

Cascade Mountains, Columbia Plateau and the Northern Rocky Mountains—each of which supports a different group of birds.

The Pacific Border province occupies the western portion of the state and includes the entire length of Washington's coastline. It also encompasses the Washington Coast Ranges, consisting of the Olympic Mountains and Willapa Hills, which are home to birds such as the Chestnut-backed Chickadee and Band-tailed Pigeon. This coastal province is also the best place to see many water birds such as the Lesser Scaup and wintering Dunlin.

The Sierra-Cascade province is dominated by the Cascade Range and its tallest peak, Mount Rainier. Paralleling the Pacific Border province, running almost due north and south through central Washington, this area is home to the Rufous Hummingbird and Downy Woodpecker.

The Columbia Plateau lies in the southeastern part of the state. It is a rolling, prairie-like region with heavy agriculture activity (wheat). This locale is home to open country birds such as the Horned Lark, and Eastern and Western Kingbirds.

In the northeastern quarter of the state are the Northern Rocky Mountains, the fourth physiographic region, with such birds as the Violet-green Swallow and Mountain Chickadee.

Varying habitats in Washington also mean variations in weather. Since elevation in the state rises from sea level along the coast to over 14,000 feet (4,250 m) at Mount Rainier, the state's highest peak, there are great differences in the weather. Tall peaks in the Cascade Mountains are some of the coldest and snowiest places in Washington, while the Columbia Plateau in the southeast is the beneficiary of warming air as it moves down from the high country. Diversity of weather is another reason why Washington is a great place to see a wide variety of birds.

Whatever the weather or elevation, there are birds to watch in each season. Whether witnessing a migration of hawks in fall or welcoming back hummingbirds in spring, there is variety and excitement in birding as each season turns to the next.

OBSERVE WITH A STRATEGY; TIPS FOR IDENTIFYING BIRDS

Identifying birds isn't as difficult as you might think. By simply following a few basic strategies, you can increase your chances of successfully identifying most birds you see! One of the first and easiest things to do when you see a new bird is to note its color. (Also, since this book is organized by color, you will go right to that color section to find it.)

Next, note the size of the bird. A strategy to quickly estimate size is to select a small-, medium- and large-sized bird to use for reference. For example, most people are familiar with robins. A robin, measured from tip of the bill to tip of the tail, is 10 inches (25 cm) long. Using the robin as an example of a medium-sized bird, select two other birds, one smaller and one larger. Many people use a House Sparrow, at about 6 inches (15 cm), and an American Crow, about 18 inches (45 cm). When you see a bird that you don't know, you can quickly ask yourself, "Is it smaller than a robin, but larger than a sparrow?" When you look in your field guide to help identify your bird, you'll know it's roughly between 6 and 10 inches (15 to 25 cm) long. This will help to narrow your choices.

Next, note the size, shape and color of the bill. Is it long, short, thick, thin, pointed, blunt, curved or straight? Seed-eating birds, such as Evening Grosbeaks, have bills that are thick and strong enough to crack even the toughest seeds. Birds that sip nectar, such as Rufous Hummingbirds, need long thin bills to reach deep into flowers. Hawks and owls tear their prey with very sharp, curving bills. Sometimes, just noting the bill shape can help you decide if the bird is a woodpecker, finch, grosbeak, blackbird or bird of prey.

Next, take a look around and note the habitat in which you see the bird. Is it wading in a saltwater marsh? Walking along a riverbank or on the beach? Soaring in the sky? Is it perched high in the trees or hopping along the forest floor? Because of their preferences in diet and habitat, you'll usually see robins hopping on the ground, but not often eating the seeds at your feeder. Or you'll see a Black-headed Grosbeak sitting on a tree branch, but not climbing down the trunk headfirst the way a nuthatch does.

Noticing what a bird is eating will give you another clue to help you identify that bird. Feeding is a big part of any bird's life. Fully one-third of all bird activity revolves around searching for and catching food, or actually eating. While birds don't always follow all the rules of what we think they eat, you can make some general assumptions. Northern Flickers, for instance, feed upon ants and other insects, so you wouldn't expect to see them visiting a backyard bird feeder. Some birds, such as the Barn Swallow and the Tree Swallow, feed on flying insects, and spend hours swooping and diving to catch a meal.

Sometimes you can identify a bird by the way it perches. Body posture can help you differentiate between an American Crow and a Red-tailed Hawk. American Crows lean forward over their feet on a branch, while hawks perch in a vertical position. Look for this the next time you see a large unidentified bird in a tree.

Birds in flight are often difficult to identify, but noting the size and shape of the wing will help. A bird's wing size is in direct proportion to its body size, weight and type of flying. The shape of the wing determines if the bird flies fast and with precision, or slowly and less precisely. Birds such as House Finches, which flit around thick tangles of branches, have short round wings. Birds that soar on warm updrafts of air, such as Turkey Vultures, have long broad wings. Barn Swallows have short pointed wings that slice through air, propelling their swift and accurate flight.

Some birds have unique flight patterns that aid in identification. American Goldfinches fly in a distinctive up-and-down pattern that makes it look as if they are riding a roller coaster.

While it's not easy to make these observations in the short time you often have to watch a "mystery bird," practicing these methods of identification will greatly expand your skills in birding. Also, seek the guidance of a more experienced birder who will help you improve your skills and answer questions on the spot.

BIRD BASICS

It's easier to identify birds and communicate about them if you know the names of the different parts of a bird. For instance, it's much easier to use the word "crest" to indicate the erect feathers on the head of a Steller's Jay than trying to describe them.

The following illustration points out the basic parts of a bird. Because it is a composite of many birds, it shouldn't be confused with any actual bird.

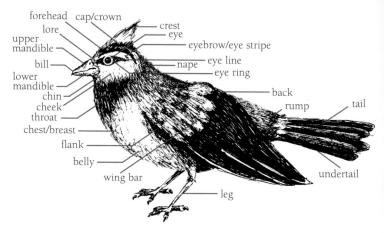

BIRD COLOR VARIABLES

No other animal has a color pallet like a bird's. Brilliant blues, lemon yellows, showy reds and iridescent greens are common-place within the bird world. In general, the male birds are more colorful than their female counterparts. This is probably to help the male attract a mate, essentially saying, "Hey, look at me!" It also calls attention to the male's overall health. The better the condition of his feathers, the better his food source and territory, and therefore, the better his potential for a mate.

Female birds that don't look like their male counterparts (such species are called sexually dimorphic, meaning "two forms") are often a nondescript color, as seen with the Lazuli Bunting. These muted tones help hide the females during weeks of motionless incubation, and draw less attention to them when they are out feeding or taking a break from the rigors of raising young.

In some species, such as the Bald Eagle, Steller's Jay and Downy Woodpecker, the male birds look nearly identical to the females. In the case of the woodpeckers, the sexes are only differentiated by a single red or sometimes yellow mark. Depending on the species, the mark may be on top of the head, face, nape of the neck or just behind the bill.

During the first year, juvenile birds often look like the mothers. Since brightly colored feathers are used mainly for attracting a mate, young non-breeding males don't have a need for colorful plumage. It is not until the first spring molt (or several years later, depending on the species) that young males obtain their breeding colors.

Both breeding and winter plumages are the result of molting. Molting is the process of dropping old worn feathers and replacing them with new ones. All birds molt, typically twice a year, with the spring molt usually occurring in late winter. During this time, most birds produce their breeding plumage (brighter colors for attracting mates), which lasts throughout the summer.

Winter plumage is the result of the late summer molt, which serves a couple of important functions. First, it adds feathers for warmth in the coming winter. Second, in some species it produces feathers that tend to be drab in color, which helps to camouflage the birds and hide them from predators. The winter plumage of the male American Goldfinch, for example, is an olive brown, unlike its obvious canary yellow color in summer. Luckily for us, some birds, such as Spotted Towhees, retain their bright summer colors all year long.

BIRD NESTS

Bird nests are truly an amazing feat of engineering. Imagine building your home strong enough to weather a storm, large enough to hold your entire family, insulated enough to shelter them from cold and heat, and waterproof enough to keep out rain. Now, build it without any blueprints or directions, and without the use of your hands or feet! Birds do!

Before building a nest, an appropriate site must be selected. With some birds, such as the House Wren, the male picks out several potential sites and assembles several small twigs in each. This discourages other birds from using nearby nest cavities. These "extra" nests are occasionally called dummy nests. The female is then taken around and shown all the choices. She chooses her favorite and finishes constructing the nest. With some other species of birds, for example, the Bullock's Oriole, it's the female who chooses the site and builds the nest with the male only offering an occasional suggestion. Each bird species has its own nest-building routine, which is strictly followed.

Nesting material usually consists of natural elements found in the immediate area. Most nests consist of plant fibers (such as bark peeled from grapevines), sticks, mud, dried grass, feathers, fur, or soft fuzzy tufts from thistle. Some birds, including Anna's Hummingbirds, use spider webs to glue nest materials together. Nesting material is limited to what a bird can hold or carry. Because of this, a bird must make many trips afield to gather enough materials to complete its nest. Most nests will take at least four days or more, and hundreds, if not thousands, of trips to build.

As you'll see in the following illustrations, birds build a wide variety of nest types.

ground nest   platform nest   cup nest   pendulous nest

The simple **ground nest** is scraped out of earth. These shallow depressions usually contain no nesting material, and are made by birds such as the Killdeer and Horned Lark.

Another kind of nest, the **platform nest**, represents a more complex type of nest building. Constructed of small twigs and branches, the platform nest is a simple arrangement of sticks which forms a platform and features a small depression to nestle the eggs.

Some platform nests, such as those of the Canada Goose, are constructed on the ground, and are made of mud and grass. Platform nests can also be on cliffs, bridges, balconies or even in flowerpots. This kind of nest gives space to adventurous young-sters, and functions as a landing platform for the parents. Many waterfowl construct platform nests on the ground, usually near water or actually in the water. These floating platform nests vary with the water level, thus preventing nests with eggs from being flooded. Platform nests, constructed by such birds as Mourning Doves and herons, are not anchored to the tree, and may tumble from the branches during high winds and storms.

The **cup nest** is a modified platform nest, used by three-quarters of all songbirds. Constructed from the outside in, a supporting platform is constructed first. This platform is attached firmly to a tree, shrub or rock ledge. Next, the sides are constructed of grasses, small twigs, bark or leaves, which are woven together and often glued with mud for additional strength. The inner cup, lined with feathers, animal fur, soft plant material or animal hair, is constructed last. The mother bird uses her chest to cast the final contours of the inner nest.

The **pendulous nest** is an unusual nest, looking more like a sock hanging from a branch than a nest. Inaccessible to most predators, these nests are attached to the ends of the smallest branches of a tree, and often wave wildly in the breeze. Woven very tightly of plant fibers, they are strong and watertight, taking up to a week to build. More commonly used by tropical birds, this complicated nest type has also been mastered by orioles and kinglets. A small opening on the top or side allows the parents access to the grass-lined interior. (It must be one heck of a ride to be inside one of these nests during a windy spring thunderstorm!)

One of the most clever of all nest types is known as the **no nest** or daycare nest. Parasitic birds, such as Brown-headed Cowbirds, build no nests at all! The egg-laden female expertly searches out other birds' nests and sneaks in to lay one of her own eggs while the host mother is not looking, thereby leaving the host mother to raise an adopted youngster. The mother cowbird wastes no energy building a nest only to have it raided by a predator. By using several nests of other birds, she spreads out her progeny in hope that at least one of her offspring will live to maturity.

Another type of nest, the **cavity nest**, is used by many birds, including woodpeckers and Western Bluebirds. The cavity nest is usually excavated in a tree branch or trunk, and offers shelter from storms, sun, predators and cold. A relatively small entrance hole in a tree leads to an inner chamber up to 10 inches (25 cm) below. Usually constructed by woodpeckers, the cavity nest is typically used only once by its builder, but subsequently can be used for many years by birds such as mergansers, Tree Swallows and bluebirds, which do not have the capability of excavating one for themselves. Kingfishers, on the other hand, excavate a tunnel up to 4 feet (1 m) long, which connects the entrance in a riverbank to the nest chamber. These cavity nests are often sparsely lined because they are already well insulated.

Some birds, including some swallows, take nest building one step further. They use a collection of small balls of mud to construct an adobe-style home. Constructed under the eaves of houses, under bridges or inside chimneys, some of these nests look like simple cup nests. Others are completely enclosed, with small tunnel-like openings that lead into a safe nesting chamber for the baby birds.

WHO BUILDS THE NEST?

In general, the female bird builds the nest. She gathers nesting materials and constructs a nest, with an occasional visit from her mate to check on the progress. In some species, both parents contribute equally to the construction of a nest. A male bird might forage for precisely the right sticks, grass or mud, but it's often the female that forms or puts together the nest. She uses her body to form the egg chamber. Rarely does the male build a nest by himself.

FLEDGING

Fledging is the interval between hatching and flight or leaving the nest. Some birds leave the nest within hours of hatching (precocial), but it might be weeks before they are able to fly. This is common with waterfowl and shorebirds. Until they start to fly, they are called fledglings. Birds that are still in the nest are called nestlings. Other baby birds are born naked and blind, and remain in the nest for several weeks (altricial).

WHY BIRDS MIGRATE

Why do birds migrate? The short answer is simple–food. Birds migrate to areas of high food concentrations. It is easier to breed where food is than where it is not. A typical migrating bird, the Western Tanager, for instance, will migrate from the tropics of Central America and Mexico to nest in forests of North America, taking advantage of the billions of newly hatched insects to feed its young. This trip is called **complete migration**.

Some birds of prey return from their complete migration to northern regions that are overflowing with small rodents, such as mice and voles, that have continued to breed in winter.

Complete migrators have a set time and pattern of migration. Each year at nearly the same time, they take off and head for a specific wintering ground. Complete migrators may travel great distances, sometimes as much as 15,000 miles (24,150 km) or more in a year. But complete migration doesn't necessarily imply flying from the cold, frozen northland to a tropical destination. The Dark-eyed Junco, for example, is a complete migrator that flies from the far reaches of Canada to spend the winter right here in Washington.

There are many interesting aspects to complete migrators. In the spring, males usually migrate several weeks before the females, arriving early to scope out possibilities for nesting sites and food sources, and to begin to defend territories. The females arrive several weeks later. In the autumn, in many species, the females and their young leave early, often up to four weeks before the adult males.

Not all migrators are the same. There are **partial migrators**, such as American Goldfinches, that usually wait until food supplies dwindle before they fly south. Unlike complete migrators, the partial migrators move only far enough south, or sometimes east and west, to find abundant food. Some years it might be only a few hundred miles, while other years it might be nearly a thousand. This kind of migration, dependent upon the weather and available food, is sometimes called **seasonal movement**.

Unlike the predictable ebbing and flowing behavior of complete migrators or partial migrators, **irruptive migrators** can move every third to fifth year, or in some cases, in consecutive years. These migrations are triggered when times are really tough and food is scarce. Red-breasted Nuthatches are a good example of irruptive migrators, because they leave their normal northern range in search of food or in response to overpopulation.

How Do Birds Migrate?

One of the many secrets of migration is fat. While we humans are fighting the battle of the bulge, birds intentionally gorge themselves to put on as much fat as possible while still being able to fly. Fat provides the greatest amount of energy per unit of weight, and in the same way that your car needs gas, birds are propelled by fat or stalled without it.

During long migratory flights, fat deposits are used up quickly, and birds need to stop to "refuel." This is when backyard bird feeding stations and undeveloped, natural spaces around our towns and cities are especially important. Some birds require up to two to three days of constant feeding to build up their fat reserves before continuing their seasonal trip.

Some birds, such as most eagles, hawks, ospreys, falcons and vultures, migrate during the day. Larger birds can hold more body fat, go longer without eating and take longer to migrate. These birds glide along on rising columns of warm air, called thermals, which hold them aloft while they slowly make their way north or south. They generally rest at night and hunt early in the morning before the sun has a chance to warm up the land and create good soaring conditions. Birds migrating during the day use a combination of landforms, rivers, and the rising and setting sun to guide them in the right direction.

Most other birds migrate during the night. Studies show that some birds which migrate at night use the stars to navigate. Others use the setting sun, while still others, such as doves, use the earth's magnetic fields to guide them north or south. While flying at night might seem like a crazy idea, nocturnal migration is safer for several reasons. First, there are fewer nighttime predators for migrating birds. Second, traveling at night allows time during the day to find food in unfamiliar surroundings. Finally, nighttime wind patterns tend to be flat, or laminar. These flat winds don't have the turbulence associated with the daytime winds, and can actually help carry smaller birds by pushing them along.

HOW TO USE THIS GUIDE

To help you quickly and easily identify birds, this book is organized by color. Simply note the color of the bird and turn to that section. Refer to the first page for the color key. For example, the male Downy Woodpecker is black and white with some red on its head. Because it is mostly black and white, it will be found in the black and white section. Each color section is also arranged by size, generally with the smaller birds first. Sections may also incorporate the average size in a range, which in some cases reflects size differences between the male and female birds. Flip through the pages in that color section to find the bird. If you already know the name of the bird, check the index for the page number. In some species, the male and female are remarkably different in color. In others, the color of the breeding and winter plumages differs. These species have an inset photograph with a page reference and in most cases are found in two color sections.

In the description section you will find a variety of information about the bird. On the next page is a sample of the information included in the book.

RANGE MAPS

Range maps are included for each bird. Colored areas indicate where in the state a particular bird is most likely to be found. Green is used for summer, blue for winter, red for year-round and yellow for areas where the bird is seen during migration. While every effort has been made to accurately depict these ranges, they are only general guidelines. Ranges actually change on an ongoing basis due to a variety of factors. Changes in weather, species abundance, landscape and vital resources such as the availability of food and water can affect local populations, migration and movements, causing birds to be found in areas not typical for the species.

Colored areas simply mean bird sightings for that species have been frequent in those areas and less frequent in the others. Please use the maps as intended–as general guides only.

COMMON NAME
Scientific name

YEAR-ROUND
MIGRATION
SUMMER
WINTER

Size: measures head to tail, may include wingspan

Male: a brief description of the male bird, and may include breeding, winter or other plumages

Female: a brief description of the female bird, which is sometimes not the same as the male

Juvenile: a brief description of the juvenile bird, which often looks like the female

Nest: the kind of nest this bird builds to raise its young, who builds the nest, and how many broods per year

Eggs: how many eggs you might expect to see in a nest, and the color of the eggs

Incubation: the average time the parents spend incubating the eggs, and who does the incubation

Fledging: the average time the young spend in the nest after hatching but before they leave the nest, and which parent(s) does most of the "child-care" and feeding

Migration: type of migration: complete (consistent, seasonal), or partial (seasonal, destination varies), or irruptive (unpredictable, depending on the food supply), or non-migrator

Food: what the bird eats most of the time (e.g., seeds, nectar, insects, fruit, small animals), and if it typically comes to a bird feeding station

Compare: notes about other birds that look similar, and the pages on which they can be found

Stan's Notes: Interesting gee-whiz natural history information. Th could be something to look or listen for, or something to help positiv identify the bird. Also includes remarkable features.

female pg. 109

male

BROWN-HEADED COWBIRD
Molothrus ater

Size: 7½" (19 cm)

Male: A glossy black bird, reminiscent of a Red-winged Blackbird. Chocolate brown head with a pointed, sharp gray bill.

Female: dull brown bird with bill similar to male

Juvenile: similar to female, only dull gray color and a streaked chest

Nest: no nest; lays eggs in nests of other birds

Eggs: 5-7; white with brown markings

Incubation: 10-13 days; host bird incubates eggs

Fledging: 10-11 days; host birds feed young

Migration: complete, to southern states

Food: insects, seeds, will come to seed feeders

Compare: The male Red-winged Blackbird (pg 9) is slightly larger, with red and yellow patches on upper wings. European Starling (pg. 5) has a shorter tail.

Stan's Notes: A member of the blackbird family. Of approximately 750 species of parasitic birds worldwide, this is the only parasitic bird in the state, laying all eggs in host birds' nests, leaving others to raise its young. Cowbirds are known to have laid eggs in nests of over 200 species of birds. Some birds reject cowbird eggs, but most raise them, even to the exclusion of their own young. Look for warblers and other birds feeding young birds twice their own size. At one time cowbirds followed bison to feed on the insect attracted to the animals.

winter

breeding

YEAR-ROUND

EUROPEAN STARLING
Sturnus vulgaris

Size: 7½" (19 cm)

Male: Iridescent purple black bird covered with white speckles during autumn and winter. Shiny purple black in spring and summer. Long, pointed yellow bill in the spring and gray in autumn. Short tail.

Female: same as male

Juvenile: similar to adult, gray brown in color with a streaked chest

Nest: cavity; male and female line the cavity; 2 broods per year

Eggs: 4-6; bluish with brown markings

Incubation: 12-14 days; female and male incubate

Fledging: 18-20 days; female and male feed young

Migration: non-migrator to partial migrator, some will move to southern states

Food: insects, seeds, fruit, comes to seed and suet feeders

Compare: Male Brown-headed Cowbird (pg. 3) has a brown head and longer tail.

Stan's Notes: A great songster, it is also able to mimic sounds. Often displaces woodpeckers, chickadees and other cavity-nesting birds. Can be very aggressive and destroy eggs or young of other birds. The bill changes color with the seasons: yellow in spring and gray in autumn. Jaws are designed to be the most powerful when opening, as they pry open crevices to locate hidden insects. Gathers in the hundreds in autumn. Not a native bird, it was introduced to New York City in 1890-91 from Europe.

male

female

SPOTTED TOWHEE
Pipilo maculatus

YEAR-ROUND
WINTER

Size: 8½" (22 cm)

Male: A mostly black bird with dirty-red-brown sides and white belly. Multiple white spots on wings and sides. Long black tail with a white tip. Rich red eyes.

Female: very similar to male, with a brown head

Juvenile: brown with heavily streaked chest

Nest: cup; female builds; 1-2 broods per year

Eggs: 3-5; white with brown markings

Incubation: 12-14 days; female and male incubate

Fledging: 10-12 days; female and male feed young

Migration: partial migrator to non-migrator

Food: seeds, fruit, insects

Compare: Fox Sparrow (pg. 101) is found in a similar habitat, but is brown and lacks the Spotted Towhee's white belly. Slightly smaller than American Robin (pg. 211).

Stan's Notes: Found in a variety of habitats, from thick brush and chaparral to suburban backyards. Often heard noisily scratching around through dead leaves on the ground in search of food. Over 70 percent of its diet is plant material, consuming more insects in the spring and summer. Well known for retreating from danger by walking away rather than taking to flight. Female builds the nest, nearly always on the ground beneath bushes, but away from where the male perches to sing. Begins breeding in April with egg laying occurring in May. After the breeding season and before winter it moves to higher elevations. Song and plumage vary geographically and are not well studied or understood.

female pg. 117

male

YEAR-ROUND

RED-WINGED BLACKBIRD
Agelaius phoeniceus

Size: 8½" (22 cm)

Male: Jet black bird with red and yellow shoulder patches on upper wings. Pointed black bill.

Female: heavily streaked brown bird with a pointed brown bill and white eyebrows

Juvenile: same as female

Nest: cup; female builds; 2-3 broods per year

Eggs: 3-4; bluish green with brown markings

Incubation: 10-12 days; female incubates

Fledging: 11-14 days; female and male feed young

Migration: non-migrator to partial migrator

Food: seeds, insects, will come to seed feeders

Compare: Slightly larger than the male Brown-headed Cowbird (pg. 3), but is less iridescent and lacks Cowbird's brown head. Differs from all blackbirds due to the red and yellow patches on its wings (epaulets).

Stan's Notes: One of the most widespread and numerous birds in the state. It is a sure sign of spring when the Red-winged Blackbirds return to the marshes. Flocks of up to 100,000 birds have been reported. Males return before the females and defend territories by singing from the tops of surrounding vegetation. Will repeat call from top of cattail while showing off its red and yellow wing bars (epaulets). Nests are usually over shallow water in thick stands of cattails. They feed mostly on seeds in spring and fall, switching to insects during summer. Females choose mate.

female pg. 119

male

BREWER'S BLACKBIRD
Euphagus cyanocephalus

YEAR-ROUND
WINTER

Size: 9" (22.5 cm)

Male: Overall glossy black, shining green in direct light. Head more purple than green. Bright yellow or pale eyes. In winter, can be dull gray to black.

Female: similar to male, only overall grayish brown with dark eyes

Juvenile: similar to female

Nest: cup; female builds; 1-2 broods per year

Eggs: 4-6; gray with brown markings

Incubation: 12-14 days; female incubates

Fledging: 13-14 days; female and male feed young

Migration: non-migrator to partial migrator

Food: insects, seeds, fruit

Compare: The male Brown-headed Cowbird (pg. 3) is smaller and has a brown head. Male Red-winged Blackbird (pg. 9) has obvious red and yellow shoulder marks.

Stan's Notes: Common blackbird of open areas such as farms, wet pastures, mountain meadows and even desert scrub. Usually nests in a shrub, small tree or directly on the ground. Prefers nesting in small colonies of up to 20 pairs. Will flock with other species such as Red-winged Blackbirds and cowbirds. A common cowbird host.

11

female pg. 123

male

YELLOW-HEADED BLACKBIRD
Xanthocephalus xanthocephalus

MIGRATION
SUMMER

Size: 9-11" (22.5-28 cm)

Male: Large black bird with a lemon-yellow head, chest and nape of neck. Black mask and a gray bill. White wing patches.

Female: similar to male, only slightly smaller with a brown body, dull yellow head and chest

Juvenile: similar to female

Nest: cup; female builds; 2 broods per year

Eggs: 3-5; greenish white with brown markings

Incubation: 11-13 days; female incubates

Fledging: 9-12 days; female feeds young

Migration: complete, to southern states and Mexico

Food: insects, seeds

Compare: Larger than the male Red-winged Blackbird (pg. 9), which has red and yellow patches on its wings. Male Yellow-headed Blackbird is the only large black bird with a bright yellow head.

Stan's Notes: Usually heard before seen, Yellow-headed Blackbird has a low, hoarse, raspy or metallic call. Nests in deep water marshes unlike its cousin, the Red-winged Blackbird, which prefers shallow water. The male gives an impressive mating display, flying with head drooped and feet and tail pointing down while steadily beating its wings. The female incubates alone and feeds between three to five young. Young keep low and out of sight for up to three weeks before starting to fly. Migrates in flocks of up to 200 with other blackbirds. Flocks made up mainly of males return first in late March and early April; females return later. Most colonies consist of 20 to 100 nests.

AMERICAN COOT
Fulica americana

Size: 13-16" (33-40 cm)

Male: Slate gray to black all over, white bill with dark band near tip. Green legs and feet. A small white patch near the base of the tail. Prominent red eyes, with a small red patch above bill between eyes.

Female: same as male

Juvenile: much paler than adult, with a gray bill and same white rump patch

Nest: floating platform; female and male build; 1 brood per year

Eggs: 9-12; pinkish buff with brown markings

Incubation: 21-25 days; female and male incubate

Fledging: 49-52 days; female and male feed young

Migration: non-migrator to partial migrator, to western coastal U.S. and Mexico, Central America

Food: insects, aquatic plants

Compare: Smaller than most waterfowl, it is the only black water bird or duck-like bird with a white bill.

Stan's Notes: An excellent diver and swimmer, often seen in large flocks on open water. Not a duck, as it doesn't have webbed feet, but instead has large lobed toes. When taking off, scrambles across surface of water with wings flapping. Bobs head while swimming. Nest is floating mat of vegetation. Huge flocks of up to 1,000 birds gather for fall migration and during winter. The unusual name is of unknown origin, but in Middle English, *coote* was used to describe various waterfowl–perhaps it stuck. Also called Mud-hen.

YEAR-ROUND

AMERICAN CROW
Corvus brachyrhynchos

Size: 18" (45 cm)

Male: All-black bird with black bill, legs and feet. Can have purple sheen in direct sunlight.

Female: same as male

Juvenile: same as adult

Nest: platform; female builds; 1 brood per year

Eggs: 4-6; bluish to olive green, brown markings

Incubation: 18 days; female incubates

Fledging: 28-35 days; female and male feed young

Migration: non-migrator to partial migrator

Food: fruit, insects, mammals, fish, carrion, will come to seed and suet feeders

Compare: Similar to the Common Raven (pg. 19), but has a smaller bill and lacks shaggy throat feathers. Crow has higher-pitched call than the Raven's deep, low raspy call. Crow has a squared tail. Raven has a wedge-shaped tail, apparent in flight. Black-billed Magpie (pg. 43) has a long tail and white belly.

Stan's Notes: One of the most recognizable birds in Washington. Often reuses its nest every year if not taken over by a Great Horned Owl. Collects and stores bright, shiny objects in the nest. Able to mimic human voices, and other birds. One of the smartest of all birds and very social, often entertaining itself by provoking chases with other birds. Feeds on road kill but is rarely hit by cars. Can live up to 20 years. Unmated birds, known as helpers, help raise young. Large extended families roost together at night, dispersing during the day to hunt.

COMMON RAVEN
Corvus corax

YEAR-ROUND

Size: 22-27" (56-69 cm)

Male: Large all-black bird with a large black bill, a shaggy beard of feathers on the chin and throat, and a large wedge-shaped tail, seen in flight.

Female: same as male

Juvenile: same as adult

Nest: platform; female and male build; 1 brood per year

Eggs: 4-6; pale green with brown markings

Incubation: 18-21 days; female incubates

Fledging: 38-44 days; female and male feed young

Migration: non-migrator to partial migrator

Food: insects, fruit, small animals, carrion

Compare: Larger than its cousin, the American Crow (pg. 17), which lacks the throat patch of feathers. Glides on flat outstretched wings, compared to the slightly V-shaped pattern of Crow. Low raspy call distinguishes the Raven from the higher-pitched Crow.

Stan's Notes: Considered by some to be the smartest of all birds. Known for its aerial acrobatics and long swooping dives. Scavenges with crows and gulls. Known to follow wolf packs around to pick up scraps and pick at bones of a kill. Complex courtship includes grabbing bills, preening each other and cooing. Mates for life. Uses same nest site for many years. Most don't breed until 3 to 4 years of age.

soaring

TURKEY VULTURE
Cathartes aura

Size: 26-32" (66-80 cm); up to 6-foot wingspan

Male: Large bird with obvious red head and legs. In flight, the wings appear two-toned: black leading edge with gray on the trailing edge and tip. The tips of wings end in finger-like projections. Squared-off tail. Ivory bill.

Female: same as male

Juvenile: same as adult, but often a gray-to-blackish head and bill

Nest: no nest, or minimal nest on cliff or in cave; 1 brood per year

Eggs: 2; white with brown markings

Incubation: 38-41 days; female and male incubate

Fledging: 66-88 days; female and male feed young

Migration: complete, to southern states, Mexico, and Central and South America

Food: carrion, just about any dead animal of any size, parents regurgitate for young

Compare: Smaller than the Bald Eagle (pg. 51), look for Vulture's two-toned wings. Flies holding wings in a slight V shape, unlike the Eagle's straight wing position.

Stan's Notes: The vulture's naked head is an adaptation to reduce the risk of feather fouling (picking up diseases) from carcasses. Unlike hawks and eagles, it has weak feet more suited to walking than grasping. One of the few birds with a developed sense of smell. Generally mute, it makes only grunts or groans. Groups often seen in trees with wings outstretched to catch sun.

drying

DOUBLE-CRESTED CORMORANT
Phalacrocorax auritus

YEAR-ROUND
MIGRATION
SUMMER

Size: 33" (84 cm)

Male: Large all-black water bird with long snake-like neck. A long yellow orange bill with a hooked tip.

Female: same as male

Juvenile: lighter brown with a grayish-colored breast and neck

Nest: platform, in colony; male and female build; 1 brood per year

Eggs: 3-4; bluish white without markings

Incubation: 25-29 days; female and male incubate

Fledging: 37-42 days; male and female feed young

Migration: partial migrator to non-migrator, to western coastal U.S.

Food: small fish, aquatic insects

Compare: Similar size as the Turkey Vulture (pg. 21), which also perches on branches with wings open to dry in sun, but lacks the Vulture's naked red head. Twice the size of American Coot (pg. 15), which lacks the Cormorant's long neck and long pointed bill.

Stan's Notes: Often seen flying in large V formation. Often roosts in large groups in trees near water. Catches fish by swimming with wings held at its sides. To dry off it strikes an erect pose with wings outstretched, facing the sun. The name refers to its nearly invisible crests. "Cormorant" comes from the Latin *corvus*, meaning "crow," and *L. marinus*, meaning "pertaining to the sea," literally, "Sea Crow."

male

female

DOWNY WOODPECKER
Picoides pubescens

YEAR-ROUND

Size: 6" (15 cm)

Male: A small woodpecker with an all-white belly, black-and-white spotted wings, a black line running through its eyes, a short black bill, a white stripe down back and a red mark on nape of neck. Several small black spots along sides of white tail.

Female: same as male, but lacks red mark on nape

Juvenile: same as female, some have a red mark near the forehead

Nest: cavity; male and female excavate; 1 brood per year

Eggs: 3-5; white without markings

Incubation: 11-12 days; female and male incubate, the female during day, male at night

Fledging: 20-25 days; male and female feed young

Migration: non-migrator

Food: insects, seeds, visits seed and suet feeders

Compare: Almost identical to the Hairy Woodpecker (pg. 33), but smaller. Look for the shorter, thinner bill of Downy to differentiate them.

Stan's Notes: Stiff tail feathers help brace this bird like a tripod as it clings to a tree. Like all woodpeckers, has long barbed tongue to pull insects from tiny places. Both sexes drum on branch or hollow log to announce territories that are rarely larger than 5 acres (2 ha). Male performs most brooding. Will winter roost in cavity. Found in the state where trees are present. Doesn't breed in high elevations, but often moves to higher elevations in summer in search of food.

YEAR-ROUND

RED-BREASTED SAPSUCKER
Sphyrapicus ruber

Size: 8½" (22 cm)

Male: Black and white body, wings and tail. Belly is white to pale yellow. Red head, chest and nape. White mark over bill.

Female: similar to male

Juvenile: similar to adult, lacking any red

Nest: cavity; female and male build; 1-2 broods per year

Eggs: 3-7; white without markings

Incubation: 12-14 days; female and male incubate

Fledging: 25-29 days; female and male feed young

Migration: non-migrator

Food: insects, tree sap, berries

Compare: The Red-naped Sapsucker (pg. 29) is very similar, but it has a black chest, and black and white on the head. The Red-breasted is found in western Washington, while Red-naped is seen in eastern Washington.

Stan's Notes: Most common sapsucker in western Washington. Most common in higher elevations, it is rare in residential areas or city parks. Will hybridize with Red-naped Sapsuckers in central Washington. An important species because their cavity nests are subsequently used by many cavity-nesting birds that don't excavate their own. Excavates nest cavities in dead or dying deciduous trees such as cottonwood, aspen, birch or willow. Drills a horizontal grid pattern of holes in deciduous trees, from which it drinks sap and eats the insects that are attracted to sap. Will also eat berries.

male

female

RED-NAPED SAPSUCKER
Sphyrapicus nuchalis

MIGRATION
SUMMER

Size: 8½" (22 cm)

Male: Black-and-white pattern on the back in two rows. Red forehead, chin and nape of neck.

Female: same as male, but has white chin and more white on back

Juvenile: brown version of adults, lacking any of the red markings

Nest: cavity; the male and female build; 1 brood per year

Eggs: 3-7; pale white without markings

Incubation: 12-13 days; female and male incubate

Fledging: 25-29 days; female and male feed young

Migration: complete, to Mexico and Central America

Food: insects, tree sap

Compare: Red-breasted Sapsucker (pg. 27) is similar, but has a red breast. The male Williamson's Sapsucker (pg. 31) is slightly larger and has a bright yellow belly.

Stan's Notes: Found in eastern Washington. Hybridizes with Red-breasted Sapsuckers in central Washington. Closely related to the Yellow-bellied Sapsucker of the eastern U.S. Often associated with aspen, willow and cottonwood trees, nearly always nesting in aspen trees where they are present. Creates several horizontal rows of holes in a tree from which sap oozes. A wide variety of birds and animals use the sap wells that sapsuckers drill. Sapsuckers lap the sap and eat the insects that are also attracted to sap. Can't suck sap as the name implies; rather, they lap it with their tongues. Some females lack the white chin that helps to differentiate the sexes.

female

male

YEAR-ROUND

WILLIAMSON'S SAPSUCKER
Sphyrapicus thyroideus

Size: 9" (22.5 cm)

Male: More black than white with a red chin and bright yellow belly. Bold white stripes just above and below the eyes. White rump and wing patches flash when in flight.

Female: finely barred black-and-white back with a brown head, yellow belly, no wing patches

Juvenile: similar to female

Nest: cavity; male builds; 1 brood per year

Eggs: 3-7; pale white without markings

Incubation: 12-14 days; male and female incubate

Fledging: 21-28 days; female and male feed young

Migration: complete, to Mexico and Central America, non-migrator in Washington

Food: insects, tree sap

Compare: Male Williamson's is similar to Red-naped and Red-breasted Sapsuckers (pp. 29 and 27, respectively), both of which have white on the back and red on the head. Female is similar to the Northern Flicker (pg. 129), but Flicker has brown back and gray head.

Stan's Notes: Largest sapsucker species with a striking difference between the males and females. Occupies conifer forests, foraging for insects and drilling sap wells nearly exclusively in conifer trees. Males drum early in spring to attract mates and to claim territories. Like the other sapsuckers, they have an irregular cadence to their drumming. The males excavate new cavities each year, but often in the same tree. Males do more incubating than females.

male

female

HAIRY WOODPECKER
Picoides villosus

YEAR-ROUND

Size: 9" (22.5 cm)

Male: Black-and-white woodpecker with a white belly, and black wings with rows of white spots. White stripe down back. Long black bill. Red mark on back of head.

Female: same as male, but lacks red spot

Juvenile: grayer version of female

Nest: cavity; female and male excavate; 1 brood per year

Eggs: 3-6; white without markings

Incubation: 11-15 days; female and male incubate, the female during day, male at night

Fledging: 28-30 days; male and female feed young

Migration: non-migrator

Food: insects, nuts, seeds, comes to seed and suet feeders

Compare: Larger than Downy Woodpecker (pg. 25), Hairy has a longer bill and lacks Downy's black spots along tail.

Stan's Notes: A common backyard bird that announces its arrival with a sharp chirp before landing on feeders. Barbed tongue helps extract insects from trees. Responsible for eating many destructive forest insects. Has tiny bristle-like feathers at base of bill to protect the nostrils from wood dust. Will drum on hollow logs, branches or stovepipes in springtime to announce its territory. Often prefers to excavate nest cavities in live aspen trees. Has a larger, more oval-shaped cavity entrance than that of Downy Woodpecker.

female pg. 135

male

BUFFLEHEAD
Bucephala albeola

Size: 13-15" (33-38 cm)

Male: A small duck with striking white sides and black back. Green purple head with a large white bonnet-like patch.

Female: brown version of male, with a brown head and white patch on cheek, just behind eyes

Juvenile: similar to female

Nest: cavity; female lines old woodpecker cavity; 1 brood per year

Eggs: 8-10; ivory to olive without markings

Incubation: 29-31 days; female incubates

Fledging: 50-55 days; female leads young to food

Migration: complete, to southern states, Mexico and Central America

Food: aquatic insects

Compare: Commonly confused with male Hooded Merganser (pg. 39), which lacks the male Bufflehead's white sides.

Stan's Notes: Common diving duck that travels with other ducks. Usually seen during migrations and winter, arriving late in August and remaining in Washington the entire winter. Most commonly found in sheltered bays and coastal harbors, it is also found inland on rivers and lakes. Nests in old woodpecker cavities. Unlike other ducks, young remain in nests for up to two days before venturing out with their mothers. Female is very territorial and remains with the same mate for many years.

female pg. 143

male

YEAR-ROUND
MIGRATION
SUMMER
WINTER

LESSER SCAUP
Aythya affinis

Size: 16-17" (40-43 cm)

Male: Appears mostly black with bold white sides and gray back. Chest and head look nearly black, but head appears purple with green highlights in direct sun. Bright yellow eyes.

Female: overall brown with dull white patch at base of light-gray bill, yellow eyes

Juvenile: same as female

Nest: ground; female builds; 1 brood per year

Eggs: 8-14; olive buff without markings

Incubation: 22-28 days; female incubates

Fledging: 45-50 days; female teaches young to feed

Migration: complete, to western coastal U.S., southern states, Mexico, Central America, northern South America

Food: aquatic plants and insects

Compare: Larger than American Coot (pg. 15), which lacks male Scaup's white sides. Look for the distinctive white sides of the male Scaup to help identify.

Stan's Notes: Common diving duck, completely submerging itself to feed on the bottom of lakes, unlike dabbling ducks which only tip forward to reach the bottom. Frequently seen in large flocks numbering in the thousands on area lakes and ponds, and along the coast in winter. When seen in flight, note the bold white stripe under the wings. A rare breeder in Washington, breeding north of the state through Alaska. Interesting baby-sitting arrangement in which the young form groups tended by one to three adult females.

female pg. 145

male

HOODED MERGANSER
Lophodytes cucullatus

YEAR-ROUND
MIGRATION
SUMMER

Size: 16-19" (40-48 cm)

Male: A sleek black-and-white bird with rusty brown sides. Crest "hood" raises to reveal large white patch. Long, thin black bill.

Female: sleek brown and rust bird with a ragged rusty crest and long, thin brown bill

Juvenile: similar to female

Nest: cavity; female lines old woodpecker hole; 1 brood per year

Eggs: 10-12; white without markings

Incubation: 32-33 days; female incubates

Fledging: 71 days; female feeds young

Migration: complete, to western coastal U.S., Mexico

Food: small fish, aquatic insects

Compare: A distinctive diving bird, look for the male's large white patch "hood" on the head and rusty-colored sides. Smaller than the male Common Merganser (pg. 247). The male Bufflehead (pg. 35) is smaller than Hooded Merganser and has white sides.

Stan's Notes: A small diving bird of shallow-water ponds, sloughs, lakes and rivers. Rarely found away from wooded areas, where it nests in natural cavities or nest boxes. The male Hooded Merganser can voluntarily raise and lower its crest to show off the large white patch on its head. The female will "dump" eggs into other female Hooded Merganser nests, resulting in 20 to 25 eggs in some nests. Mergansers have been known to share a nesting cavity with Wood Ducks sitting side by side.

male

female

PILEATED WOODPECKER
Dryocopus pileatus

YEAR-ROUND

Size: 19" (48 cm)

Male: Crow-sized woodpecker with a black back and bright red crest. Long gray bill with red mustache. White leading edge of the wings flashes brightly when flying.

Female: same as male, but has a black forehead and lacks red mustache

Juvenile: similar to adults, only duller and browner overall

Nest: cavity; male and female excavate; 1 brood per year

Eggs: 3-5; white without markings

Incubation: 15-18 days; female and male incubate, the female during day, male at night

Fledging: 26-28 days; female and male feed young

Migration: non-migrator

Food: insects, will come to suet feeders

Compare: This bird is quite distinctive and unlikely to be confused with any others. Look for the Pileated Woodpecker's bright red crest and exceptionally large size.

Stan's Notes: Our largest woodpecker, it excavates long oval holes up to several feet long in tree trunks, searching for insects. Large chips of wood lay at bases of excavated trees. Will drum on hollow branches, chimneys, etc., to announce territory. Relatively shy bird that prefers large tracts of woodland. Its favorite food is carpenter ants. Young are fed regurgitated insects.

41

BLACK-BILLED MAGPIE
Pica hudsonia

Size: 20" (50 cm)

Male: A large black-and-white bird with very long tail and white belly. Iridescent green wings and tail in direct sunlight. Large black bill and legs. White wing patches flash in flight.

Female: same as male

Juvenile: same as adult, but shorter tail

Nest: modified pendulous; the female and male build; 1 brood per year

Eggs: 5-8; green with brown markings

Incubation: 16-21 days; female incubates

Fledging: 25-29 days; female and male feed young

Migration: non-migrator

Food: insects, carrion, fruit, seeds

Compare: Contrasting black-and-white colors and the very long tail of Magpie distinguish it from the all-black American Crow (pg. 17).

Stan's Notes: A wonderfully intelligent bird that is able to mimic dogs, cats and even people. Will often raid a barnyard dog dish for food. Feeds on a variety of food from road kill to insects and seeds it collects from the ground. Easily identified by its bold black-and-white colors and long streaming tail. Travels in small flocks, usually family members, and tends to be very gregarious. Breeds in small colonies with unusual dome nest (dome-shaped roof) deep within thick shrubs. Will mate with same mate for several years. Prefers open fields with cattle or sheep, where it feeds on insects attracted to the livestock.

rushing

weed dance

WESTERN GREBE
Aechmophorus occidentalis

Size: 24" (60 cm)

Male: A long-necked, nearly all-black water bird with a white throat. Long yellow bill with bright red eyes. Dark cap extends around eyes to base of bill. During winter, becomes light gray around eyes.

Female: same as male

Juvenile: similar to adult

Nest: platform; female and male build; 1 brood per year

Eggs: 3-4; bluish white with brown markings

Incubation: 20-23 days; female and male incubate

Fledging: 65-75 days; female and male feed young

Migration: complete, to western coastal U.S.

Food: fish, aquatic insects

Compare: A familiar long-necked water bird. Striking black and white plumage makes it hard to confuse with any other bird.

Stan's Notes: Well known for its unusual breeding dance known as rushing. Side by side, with necks outstretched, mates will spring to their webbed feet and dance across the water's surface (see inset), diving underwater at the end of the rush. Often holds long stalks of water plants in bill when courting mate, called the weed dance (see inset). Its legs are positioned far back on the body, making it difficult to walk on ground. Shortly after choosing a large lake for breeding and till late in summer, it rarely flies. Young ride on backs of adults, climbing on only minutes after hatching. Nests in large colonies of up to 100 pairs on lakes with lots of tall vegetation.

soaring

OSPREY
Pandion haliaetus

Size: 24" (60 cm); up to 6-foot wingspan

Male: Large eagle-like bird with white chest, belly and black brown back. White head with a black streak across eyes. Large wings with black "wrist" marks.

Female: same as male, but with a necklace of brown streaking

Juvenile: similar to adults, with a light tan breast

Nest: platform; female and male build; 1 brood per year

Eggs: 2-4; white with brown markings

Incubation: 32-42 days; female and male incubate

Fledging: 48-58 days; male and female feed young

Migration: complete, to Mexico, Central America and South America

Food: fish

Compare: Bald Eagle (pg. 51) is on average 10 inches (25 cm) larger, with an all-white head and tail. The juvenile Bald Eagle is brown with white speckles. Look for a white belly and dark stripe across eyes to identify Osprey.

Stan's Notes: Ospreys are in a family all their own. It is the only raptor that will plunge into the water to catch fish. Can hover for several seconds before diving. Carries fish in a head-first position during flight for better aerodynamics. In flight, wings are angled (cocked) backward. Nests on man-made towers and tall dead trees. Recent studies show that male and female might mate for life, but don't migrate to the same wintering grounds.

winter

breeding

COMMON LOON
Gavia immer

MIGRATION
SUMMER
WINTER

Size: 28-36" (71-90 cm)

Male: Large, familiar black-and-white bird of the lakes. The breeding adult has checkerboard back with white necklace, black head and deep red eyes with long, pointed black bill. Winter has an entirely gray body and bill.

Female: same as male

Juvenile: gray version of adult, without red eyes

Nest: platform, on the ground; female and male build; 1 brood per year

Eggs: 2; olive brown, occasionally brown markings

Incubation: 26-31 days; female and male incubate

Fledging: 75-80 days; female and male feed young

Migration: complete, western coastal U.S. and Mexico, southern states

Food: fish, aquatic insects

Compare: Double-crested Cormorant (pg. 23) has a yellow bill and black chest.

Stan's Notes: A winter resident on the coast beginning in October, lasting until March. Some non-breeding adults remain all summer. Prefers clear lakes because it hunts for fish by eyesight. Legs are set so far back that it has a hard time walking on land, but it's a great swimmer. Its name comes from the Swedish word *lom*, meaning "lame," for the awkward way it walks on land. Its unique call suggests the wild laughter of a demented person, and led to the phrase "crazy as a loon." Young ride on the backs of swimming parents. Adults perform distraction displays to protect young. Very sensitive to disturbance during nesting and will abandon nest.

soaring

juvenile

BALD EAGLE
Haliaeetus leucocephalus

YEAR-ROUND
WINTER

Size: 31-37" (79-94 cm); up to 7-foot wingspan

Male: Pure white head and tail contrast with dark brown-to-black body and wings. A large, curved yellow bill and yellow feet.

Female: same as male, only slightly larger

Juvenile: dark brown with white spots or speckles throughout body and wings, gray bill

Nest: massive platform; female and male build; 1 brood per year

Eggs: 2; off-white without markings

Incubation: 34-36 days; female and male incubate

Fledging: 75-90 days; female and male feed young

Migration: partial to non-migrator in Washington

Food: fish, carrion, ducks

Compare: Golden Eagle (pg. 175) and Turkey Vulture (pg. 21) lack the white head and white tail of adult Bald Eagle. Juvenile Golden Eagle, with its white wrist marks and white base of tail, is similar to the juvenile Bald Eagle.

Stan's Notes: Often seen soaring, this bird is making a comeback in Washington. Returns to the same nest every year, adding more sticks, enlarging it to massive proportions, at times up to 1,000 pounds (450 kg). In the midair mating ritual, one eagle will flip upside down, locking talons with another. Then both tumble until they break apart to continue flying. Thought to mate for life, but will switch mates if not successful reproducing. Juveniles attain the white head and tail at about 4 to 5 years of age.

TREE SWALLOW
Tachycineta bicolor

Size: 5-6" (13-15 cm)

Male: Blue green in the spring and greener in fall. Appears to change color in direct sunlight. A white belly, a notched tail and pointed wing tips.

Female: similar to male, only duller

Juvenile: gray brown with a white belly and grayish breast band

Nest: cavity; female and male line former woodpecker cavity or nest box; 1 brood per year

Eggs: 4-6; white without markings

Incubation: 13-16 days; female incubates

Fledging: 20-24 days; female and male feed young

Migration: complete, to Mexico and Central America

Food: insects

Compare: Barn Swallow (pg. 61) has a rust belly and deeply forked tail. Similar size as the Cliff Swallow (pg. 89) and Violet-green Swallow (pg. 241), but lacks any tan-to-rust color of the Cliff Swallow and any emerald green of the Violet-green Swallow.

Stan's Notes: The first swallow species to return each spring. Most common along ponds, lakes and agricultural fields. Is attracted to your yard with a nest box. Competes with Western and Mountain Bluebirds for cavities and nest boxes. Travels great distances to find dropped feathers to line its grass nest. Sometimes seen playing, chasing after dropped feathers. Often seen flying back and forth across fields, feeding on insects. Gathers in large flocks to migrate.

female pg. 87

male

MIGRATION
SUMMER

LAZULI BUNTING
Passerina amoena

Size: 5½" (14 cm)

Male: A turquoise blue head, neck, back and tail. Cinnamon chest with cinnamon extending down flanks slightly. White belly. Two bold white wing bars. Non-breeding male has a spotty blue head and back.

Female: overall grayish brown, warm-brown breast, a light wash of blue on wings and tail, gray throat, a light gray belly, two narrow white wing bars

Juvenile: similar to adult of the same sex

Nest: cup; female builds; 2-3 broods per year

Eggs: 3-5; pale blue without markings

Incubation: 11-13 days; female incubates

Fledging: 10-12 days; female and male feed young

Migration: complete, to Mexico

Food: insects, seeds

Compare: Smaller than the male Western Bluebird (pg. 57), not as dark blue in color and chest is browner.

Stan's Notes: More common in low elevation shrub lands in the eastern portion of the state, less common in western Washington. Doesn't like dense forests. Has a strong association with water such as rivers and streams. Gathers in small flocks and tends to move up in elevations after breeding to hunt for insects and search for seeds. Has increased in populations and expanded its range over the last 100 years.

male

female

YEAR-ROUND
MIGRATION
SUMMER

WESTERN BLUEBIRD
Sialia mexicana

Size: 7" (18 cm)

Male: Deep blue head, neck, back, wings and tail. Rusty red chest and flanks.

Female: similar to male, only duller with gray head

Juvenile: similar to female, with a speckled chest

Nest: cavity, old woodpecker cavity, wooden nest box; female builds; 1-2 broods per year

Eggs: 4-6; pale blue without markings

Incubation: 13-14 days; female incubates

Fledging: 22-23 days; female and male feed young

Migration: partial to non-migrator in Washington

Food: insects, fruit

Compare: Mountain Bluebird (pg. 59) is similar, but lacks the rusty red breast. Larger than male Lazuli Bunting (pg. 55), which has white wing bars.

Stan's Notes: More common in western Washington. Found in a variety of habitats, from agricultural land to clear-cuts. Wherever it is, it requires a cavity for nesting. West of the Cascades it competes with starlings for nesting cavities. Like Mountain Bluebirds, Western Bluebirds use nesting boxes, which are responsible for the stable populations. A courting male will fly in front of female, spreading wings and tail, then perch next to her. Often seen going in and out of nest box or cavity as if to say, "Look inside." Male may offer food to female to establish pair bond.

male

female

MOUNTAIN BLUEBIRD
Sialia currucoides

Size: 7" (18 cm)

Male: An overall sky blue with darker blue back, wings, tail and head.

Female: similar to male, only paler with nearly gray head, chest and white belly

Juvenile: similar to adult of the same sex

Nest: cavity, old woodpecker cavity, wooden nest box; female builds; 1-2 broods per year

Eggs: 4-6; pale blue without markings

Incubation: 13-14 days; female incubates

Fledging: 22-23 days; female and male feed young

Migration: complete, to California, Arizona, Mexico

Food: insects

Compare: Similar to Western Bluebird (pg. 57), but not as dark blue and lacks Western's rusty red chest.

Stan's Notes: Common in open mountainous country, nesting in the eastern two-thirds of the state. Due to conservation of suitable nesting sites (dead trees with cavities and man-made nest boxes), populations have increased dramatically. Like the other bluebirds, Mountain Bluebirds take well to nest boxes and will tolerate close contact with humans. Young will imprint on their first nest box or cavity, then choose a similar type of box or cavity throughout the rest of life.

BARN SWALLOW
Hirundo rustica

Size: 7" (18 cm)

Male: A sleek swallow with a blue black back, a cinnamon belly and a reddish brown chin. White spots on long forked tail.

Female: same as male, only slightly duller

Juvenile: similar to adults, with a tan belly and chin, and shorter tail

Nest: cup; female and male build; 2 broods a year

Eggs: 4-5; white with brown markings

Incubation: 13-17 days; female incubates

Fledging: 18-23 days; female and male feed young

Migration: complete, to South America

Food: insects, prefers beetles, wasps and flies

Compare: Tree Swallow (pg. 53) has a white belly and chin, and notched tail. Larger than the Cliff Swallow (pg. 89) and Violet-green Swallow (pg. 241), which both lack the distinctive, deeply forked tail. Violet-green Swallow is distinctively green with a white face.

Stan's Notes: Of the seven swallow species in the state, this is the only one with a deeply forked tail. Unlike other swallows, the Barn Swallow rarely glides in flight, so look for continuous flapping. It builds a mud nest using up to 1,000 beak-loads of mud, often in or on barns. Nests in colonies of four to six, but nesting alone is not uncommon. Drinks while flying by skimming water or getting water from wet leaves. It also bathes while flying through the rain or sprinklers.

STELLER'S JAY
Cyanocitta stelleri

Size: 11" (28 cm)

Male: Dark blue wings, tail and belly. Black head, nape of the neck and chest. Large, pointed black crest on head that can be lifted at will.

Female: same as male

Juvenile: similar to adult

Nest: cup; female and male build; 1 brood a year

Eggs: 3-5; pale green with brown markings

Incubation: 14-16 days; female incubates

Fledging: 16-18 days; female and male feed young

Migration: non-migrator

Food: insects, berries, seeds, will visit seed feeders

Compare: The Western Scrub-Jay (pg. 65) lacks the Steller's all-black head and black crest. The Gray Jay (pg. 215) lacks any blue coloring and a crest.

Stan's Notes: Common resident of conifer forest from sea level to timberline. Often found in suburban yards, it rarely competes with Gray Jays, which occupy higher elevations. Thought to mate for life, rarely dispersing far, usually breeding within 10 miles (16 km) of the place of birth. Several subspecies found throughout the West. Washington form (shown) has a black crest and lacks any distinct white streaks on the head.

WESTERN SCRUB-JAY
Aphelocoma californica

Size: 11" (28 cm)

Male: Head, wings, tail and breast band are deep blue. Brownish patch on back. Chin, breast and belly are dull white. Very long tail.

Female: same as male

Juvenile: similar to adult, overall gray with light blue wings and tail

Nest: cup; female and male build; 1 brood a year

Eggs: 3-6; pale green with red brown markings

Incubation: 15-17 days; female incubates

Fledging: 18-20 days; female and male feed young

Migration: non-migrator

Food: insects, seeds, fruit, comes to seed feeders

Compare: Same size as Steller's Jay (pg. 63), but lacks the all-black head and pointed black crest of Steller's. Gray Jay (pg. 215) is gray and white, lacking any of Scrub-Jay's blue color.

Stan's Notes: A tame bird of urban areas that visits feeders. Several subspecies occur with some regional variations in color, the Pacific race (shown) being the deepest blue. Forms a long-term pair bond, with the male feeding female before and during incubation. Young of a pair remain close by for up to a couple years, helping parents raise subsequent brothers and sisters. Caches food by burying it for later consumption. Likely serves as a major distributor of oaks and pines by not returning to eat the seeds it buried.

male

female

YEAR-ROUND

BELTED KINGFISHER
Ceryle alcyon

Size: 13" (33 cm)

Male: Large blue bird with white belly. Broad blue gray breast band and a ragged crest that is raised and lowered at will. Large head with a long, thick black bill. A small white spot directly in front of red brown eyes. Black wing tips with splashes of white that flash when flying.

Female: same as male, but with rusty breast band in addition to blue gray band, and rusty flanks

Juvenile: similar to female

Nest: cavity; female and male excavate; 1 brood per year

Eggs: 6-7; white without markings

Incubation: 23-24 days; female and male incubate

Fledging: 23-24 days; female and male feed young

Migration: non-migrator in Washington

Food: small fish

Compare: Larger than the Western Scrub-Jay (pg. 65), which lacks Kingfisher's obvious large crest. Kingfisher is rarely found away from water.

Stan's Notes: Seen perched on branches near the water, it dives headfirst for small fish and returns to a branch to eat. Has a loud machine-gun-like call. Excavates a deep cavity in bank of river or lake. Parents drop dead fish into water, teaching young to dive. Regurgitates pellets of bone after meals, being unable to pass bones through digestive tract. Mates recognize each other by call.

YEAR-ROUND

CHESTNUT-BACKED CHICKADEE
Poecile rufescens

Size: 4¾" (12 cm)

Male: Rich, warm chestnut back and sides. Black cap and chin, with white cheeks and sides of head. Gray wings and tail.

Female: same as male

Juvenile: same as adult

Nest: cavity; female and male build; 1-2 broods per year

Eggs: 5-7; white without markings

Incubation: 10-12 days; female incubates

Fledging: 13-16 days; female and male feed young

Migration: non-migrator

Food: insects, seeds, fruit, comes to seed and suet feeders

Compare: The Black-capped Chickadee (pg. 191) and Mountain Chickadee (pg. 193) are similar, but both lack Chestnut-backed's distinctive chestnut-colored back.

Stan's Notes: The most colorful of all chickadees. Like the other chickadee species, the Chestnut-backed clings to branches upside down, looking for insects. During breeding, it is quiet and secretive. In winter it joins other birds such as kinglets, nuthatches and other chickadees. Prefers humid coastal conifer forest with hemlock and Tamarack. Uses a cavity nest from 2 to 20 feet (up to 6 m) off the ground. Will use the same nest year after year. Comes to seed and suet feeders.

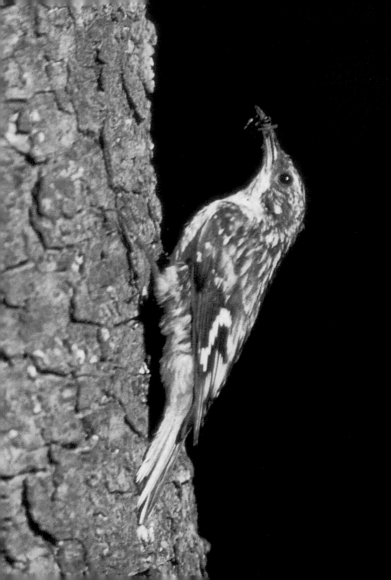

BROWN CREEPER
Certhia americana

YEAR-ROUND
WINTER

Size: 5" (13 cm)

Male: A small, thin, nearly camouflaged bird with white belly, long stiff tail and thin curved bill. Obvious white line above dark eyes.

Female: same as male

Juvenile: same as adult

Nest: cup; female builds; unknown how many broods per year

Eggs: 5-6; white with tiny brown markings

Incubation: 14-17 days; female incubates, male feeds female during incubation

Fledging: 13-16 days; female and male feed young

Migration: partial migrator to non-migrator

Food: insects, nuts, seeds

Compare: Creeps up tree trunks, not down, like the White-breasted Nuthatch (pg. 197). Watch for Creeper to fly from the top of one trunk to the bottom of another, working its way to the top, looking for insects. Slightly larger than the Red-breasted Nuthatch (pg. 187), with a similar white stripe above eyes, but Creeper has a white belly, long tail and no black crown.

Stan's Notes: Utilizes its camouflage coloring to defend itself by spreading out flat on a branch or tree trunk without moving. The young are able to follow the parents, creeping soon after fledging. Commonly seen in wooded areas. Often builds nest behind loose bark of dead or dying trees.

HOUSE WREN
Troglodytes aedon

SUMMER

Size: 5" (13 cm)

Male: A small all-brown bird with lighter brown marking on tail and wings. Brown, slightly curved bill. Often holds its tail erect.

Female: same as male.

Juvenile: same as adult

Nest: cavity; female and male line just about any cavity; 2 broods per year

Eggs: 4-6; tan with brown markings

Incubation: 10-13 days; female and male incubate

Fledging: 12-15 days; female and male feed young

Migration: complete, to southern states and Mexico

Food: insects

Compare: Bewick's Wren (pg. 83) has white eyebrows and white spots on the tail.

Stan's Notes: A prolific songster, it will sing from dawn until dusk during the mating season. Easily attracted to nest boxes. In spring, the male chooses several prospective nesting cavities and places a few small twigs in each. Female inspects each, chooses one, and finishes the nest building. She will completely fill the nest cavity with uniformly small twigs, then line a small depression at back of cavity with pine needles and grass. Often has trouble fitting long twigs through nest cavity hole. Tries many different directions and approaches until successful.

PINE SISKIN
Carduelis pinus

Size: 5" (13 cm)

Male: A small brown finch with heavily streaked back, breast and belly. Yellow wing bars and yellow at base of tail. Thin bill.

Female: same as male

Juvenile: similar to adult, with a light yellow tinge throughout chest and chin

Nest: modified cup; the female builds; 2 broods per year

Eggs: 3-4; greenish blue with brown markings

Incubation: 12-13 days; female incubates

Fledging: 14-15 days; female and male feed young

Migration: irruptive, moves around the state in search of food

Food: seeds, insects, will come to seed feeders

Compare: Female American Goldfinch (pg. 287) lacks streaks and has white wing bars. Female House Finch (pg. 77) has streaked chest, but lacks yellow wing bars. Female Purple Finch (pg. 93) has bold white eyebrows.

Stan's Notes: A widespread nesting resident throughout the state in conifer forests. Nests mostly in the western half of Washington, with nests often only a few feet apart. Builds nest toward the ends of conifer branches, where needles are dense, helping to conceal. Breeds in small groups. Male feeds the female during incubation. Juveniles lose yellow tint on chest and chin by late summer of first year. Gathers in flocks in autumn, moves around Washington and visits bird feeders.

male pg. 259

female

HOUSE FINCH
Carpodacus mexicanus

YEAR-ROUND

Size: 5" (13 cm)

Female: A plain brown bird with a heavily streaked white chest.

Male: orange red face, chest and rump, a brown cap, brown marking behind eyes, brown wings streaked with white, streaked belly

Juvenile: similar to female

Nest: cup, sometimes in cavities; female builds; 2 broods per year

Eggs: 4-5; pale blue, lightly marked

Incubation: 12-14 days; female incubates

Fledging: 15-19 days; female and male feed young

Migration: non-migrator to partial migrator, will move around to find food

Food: seeds, fruit, leaf buds, will visit seed feeders

Compare: Female Cassin's Finch (pg. 95) has a more heavily streaked belly. Similar to Pine Siskin (pg. 75), but lacks yellow wing bars and has a larger bill. Very similar female Purple Finch (pg. 93) has bold white eyebrows.

Stan's Notes: Very social bird. Visits feeders in small flocks. Likes nesting in hanging flower baskets. Incubating female fed by male. Loud, cheerful warbling song. Suffers a fatal eye disease that causes eyes to crust over. Historically it occurred from the Pacific coast to the Rocky Mountains, with only a few reaching the eastern side. House Finches introduced to Long Island, New York, in the 1940s from western America have since populated the entire eastern U.S. Now found throughout the country.

CHIPPING SPARROW
Spizella passerina

Size: 5" (13 cm)

Male: Small gray brown sparrow with a clear gray chest, rusty crown, white eyebrows with a black eye line, thin gray black bill and two faint wing bars.

Female: same as male

Juvenile: similar to adult, with a streaked breast and lacking rusty cap

Nest: cup; female builds; 2 broods per year

Eggs: 3-5; blue green with brown markings

Incubation: 11-14 days; female incubates

Fledging: 10-12 days; female and male feed young

Migration: complete, to southern states, Mexico and Central America

Food: insects, seeds, will come to ground feeders

Compare: Fox Sparrow (pg. 101) is larger and much darker brown. Smaller than Song Sparrow (pg. 81), which has heavy dark streaks on the chest. The female House Finch (pg. 77) also has a streaked chest.

Stan's Notes: A common garden or yard bird, often seen feeding on dropped seeds below feeders. Gathers in large family groups to feed each autumn in preparation for migration. Migrates at night in flocks of 20 to 30 birds. Received its common name from the male's slow "chip" call. Often just called Chippy. Nest is placed low in dense shrubs and is almost always lined with animal hair.

SONG SPARROW
Melospiza melodia

YEAR-ROUND

Size: 5-6" (13-15 cm)

Male: Common brown sparrow with heavy dark streaks on breast coalescing into a central dark spot.

Female: same as male

Juvenile: similar to adult, finely streaked chest without central spot

Nest: cup; female builds; 2 broods per year

Eggs: 3-4; pale blue to green with reddish brown markings

Incubation: 12-14 days; female incubates

Fledging: 9-12 days; female and male feed young

Migration: complete, to southern states, non-migrator in Washington

Food: insects, seeds, rarely visits seed feeders

Compare: Similar to other brown sparrows. Look for a heavily streaked chest with central dark spot.

Stan's Notes: Many Song Sparrow subspecies or varieties, but dark central spot carries through each variant. While the female builds another nest for second brood, the male often takes over feeding the young. Returns to similar area each year, defending a small territory by singing from thick shrubs. Common host of the Brown-headed Cowbird. Ground feeders, look for them to scratch simultaneously with both feet to expose seeds. Unlike many sparrow species, Song Sparrows rarely flock together.

BEWICK'S WREN
Thryomanes bewickii

YEAR-ROUND

Size: 5½" (14 cm)

Male: Brown cap, back, wings and tail. Gray chest and belly. White chin and eyebrows. Long tail with white spots on edges is cocked and flits sideways. Pointed down-curved bill.

Female: same as male

Juvenile: similar to adult

Nest: cavity; female and male build nest in woodpecker hole or nest box; 2-3 broods a year

Eggs: 4-8; white with brown markings

Incubation: 12-14 days; female incubates

Fledging: 10-14 days; female and male feed young

Migration: non-migrator to partial migrator, will move around to find food

Food: insects, seeds

Compare: House Wren (pg. 73) is smaller, and lacks the obvious white eyebrow markings and white spots on tail.

Stan's Notes: A common wren of backyards and gardens. Insects make up 97 percent of its diet, with plant seeds composing the rest. Competes with the House Wren for nest cavities. Male will choose nesting cavities and start to build nests using small uniform-sized sticks. Female will make the final selection of a nest site and finish building. Begins breeding in April and has two to three broods per year. Male feeds female while she incubates. Average size territory per pair is 5 acres (2 ha), which they defend all year long. Birds that breed in higher elevations retreat to lower elevations for the winter. Has been expanding its range in eastern Washington.

male pg. 195

female

gray-headed

Oregon female

DARK-EYED JUNCO
Junco hyemalis

YEAR-ROUND
WINTER

Size: 5½" (14 cm)

Female: A round, dark-eyed bird with tan-to-brown chest, head and back. White belly. Ivory-to-pink bill. Since the outermost tail feathers are white, tail appears as a white V in flight.

Male: same as female, only slate gray to charcoal

Juvenile: similar to female, but has a streaked breast and head

Nest: cup; female and male build; 2 broods a year

Eggs: 3-5; white with reddish brown markings

Incubation: 12-13 days; female incubates

Fledging: 10-13 days; male and female feed young

Migration: partial migrator to non-migrator

Food: seeds, insects, will come to seed feeders

Compare: Rarely confused with any other bird. Large flocks come to feed under bird feeders.

Stan's Notes: Several junco species have now been combined into one, simply called Dark-eyed Junco (see inset photos). A common and widespread nester in forested areas of the state. Very common in most cities during winter, rare during nesting season. Nests in a wide variety of wooded habitats in April and May. Usually seen on the ground in small flocks. It adheres to a rigid social hierarchy, with dominant birds chasing the less dominant birds. Look for its white outer tail feathers flashing in flight. Most comfortable on the ground, juncos will "double-scratch" with both feet to expose seeds and insects. Consumes many weed seeds.

male pg. 55

female

LAZULI BUNTING
Passerina amoena

Size: 5½" (14 cm)

Female: Overall grayish brown with a warm-brown chest, light wash of blue on wings and tail, gray throat and light gray belly. Two narrow white wing bars.

Male: turquoise blue head, neck, back and tail, cinnamon chest, white belly and two bold white wing bars

Juvenile: similar to adult of the same sex

Nest: cup; female builds; 2-3 broods per year

Eggs: 3-5; pale blue without markings

Incubation: 11-13 days; female incubates

Fledging: 10-12 days; female and male feed young

Migration: complete, to Mexico

Food: insects, seeds

Compare: The female Western Bluebird (pg. 57) and Mountain Bluebird (pg. 59) are larger, with both showing much more blue than the female Bunting.

Stan's Notes: More common in low elevation shrub lands in the eastern portion of the state, less common in western Washington. Doesn't like dense forests. Has a strong association with water such as rivers and streams. Gathers in small flocks and tends to move up in elevations after breeding to hunt for insects and search for seeds. Has increased in populations and expanded its range over the last 100 years.

SUMMER

CLIFF SWALLOW
Petrochelidon pyrrhonota

Size: 5½" (14 cm)

Male: A uniquely patterned swallow with a dark back, wings and cap. Distinctive tan-to-rust rump, cheeks and forehead.

Female: same as male

Juvenile: similar to adult, lacks distinct patterning

Nest: gourd-shaped, made of mud; the male and female build; 1-2 broods per year

Eggs: 3-6; pale white with brown markings

Incubation: 14-16 days; male and female incubate

Fledging: 21-24 days; female and male feed young

Migration: complete, to South America

Food: insects

Compare: Smaller than Barn Swallow (pg. 61), which has a blue back and wings, and a deeply forked tail. The Tree Swallow (pg. 53) lacks any tan-to-rust coloring. The Violet-green Swallow (pg. 241) is green with a bright white face.

Stan's Notes: A common and widespread species in Washington. Common around bridges and rural housing, especially in open country close to cliffs. Builds gourd-shaped nest with a funnel-like entrance pointing down. A colony nester, with many nests lined up under eves of buildings or under cliff overhangs. Will carry balls of mud up to a mile to construct nest. Many of the colony return to the same nest sites every year. Not unusual to have two broods per season. If the number of nests under eves becomes a problem, wait until after young have left the nests to hose off the mud.

HOUSE SPARROW
Passer domesticus

YEAR-ROUND

Size: 6" (15 cm)

Male: Medium sparrow-like bird with large black spot on throat extending down to the chest. Brown back and single white wing bars. A gray belly and crown.

Female: all-light-brown bird, slightly smaller, lacks the black throat patch and single wing bars

Juvenile: similar to female

Nest: domed cup nest, within cavity; female and male build; 2-3 broods per year

Eggs: 4-6; white with brown markings

Incubation: 10-12 days; female incubates

Fledging: 14-17 days; female and male feed young

Migration: non-migrator, moves around to find food

Food: seeds, insects, fruit, comes to seed feeders

Compare: The Chipping Sparrow (pg. 79) has a rusty crown. Look for the male House Sparrow's black bib. Female has a clear breast and no marking on head (cap).

Stan's Notes: One of the first bird songs heard in cities in spring. Familiar city bird, nearly always in flocks. Introduced from Europe to Central Park, New York, in 1850 and now found throughout North America. These birds are not really sparrows, but members of the Weaver Finch family, characterized by their large, oversized domed nests. Constructs a nest containing scraps of plastic, paper and whatever else is available. An aggressive bird that will kill the young of other birds in order to take over a cavity.

male pg. 261

female

PURPLE FINCH
Carpodacus purpureus

YEAR-ROUND
WINTER

Size: 6" (15 cm)

Female: A plain brown bird with a heavily streaked chest. Prominent white eyebrows.

Male: raspberry-red head, cap, breast, back and rump, brownish wings and tail

Juvenile: same as female

Nest: cup; female and male build; 1 brood a year

Eggs: 4-5; greenish blue with brown markings

Incubation: 12-13 days; female incubates

Fledging: 13-14 days; female and male feed young

Migration: irruptive, moves around in search of food

Food: seeds, insects, fruit, comes to seed feeders

Compare: Female House Finch (pg. 77) lacks female Purple Finch's white eyebrows. Pine Siskin (pg. 75) has yellow wing bars and a much smaller bill than Purple Finch. The female American Goldfinch (pg. 287) has a clear chest and white wing bars.

Stan's Notes: A year-round resident, common in non-residential areas. Preferring open woods or woodland edges of low to middle elevation conifer forest, it has been replaced in cities by the House Finch. Feeds primarily on seeds, with the seeds of ash trees a very important food source. Will come to seed feeders along with House Finches, making it hard to tell them apart. A rich loud song, with a distinctive "tic" note made only in flight. Travels in flocks of up to 50. Nests in May. Not a purple color, the Latin name *purpureus* means "crimson" or other reddish color.

female

male pg. 263

CASSIN'S FINCH
Carpodacus cassinii

Size: 6½" (16 cm)

Female: Brown-to-gray finch with fine black streaks on back and wings. Heavily streaked white chest and belly.

Male: light wash of crimson red, especially bright red crown, brown streaks on the back and wings, white belly

Juvenile: similar to female

Nest: cup; female builds; 1-2 broods per year

Eggs: 3-5; white without markings

Incubation: 12-14 days; female incubates

Fledging: 14-18 days; female and male feed young

Migration: partial migrator to non-migrator, will move around to find food

Food: seeds, insects, fruits, berries, will visit seed feeders

Compare: The female House Finch (pg. 77) is similar, but has a gray belly that is not as streaked.

Stan's Notes: A common mountain finch of eastern Washington's conifer forests. Usually forages for seeds on the ground, but also eats evergreen buds, and aspen and willow catkins. Breeds in May. Colony nester, depending on the regional food source. The more food available, the larger the colony. Male sings a fast warble, often imitating other birds such as jays, tanagers and grosbeaks. Even though it is a cowbird host, its population has increased over the past 20 years.

juvenile

YEAR-ROUND
WINTER

WHITE-CROWNED SPARROW
Zonotrichia leucophrys

Size: 6½-7½" (16-19 cm)

Male: A brown sparrow with a gray breast and a black-and-white striped crown. Small, thin pink bill.

Female: same as male

Juvenile: similar to adult, with brown stripes on the head instead of white

Nest: cup; female builds; 2 broods per year

Eggs: 3-5; varies between greenish, bluish and whitish, with red brown markings

Incubation: 11-14 days; female incubates

Fledging: 8-12 days; male and female feed young

Migration: complete, to western coastal U.S., southern states and Mexico

Food: insects, seeds, berries, visits ground feeders

Compare: The Golden-crowned Sparrow (pg. 99) has a central yellow spot on the crown.

Stan's Notes: Year-round resident in the western half of the state. Usually seen in groups of up to 20 during the winter, when groups gather to move around and search for food. Males establish their territories by singing from perches. Nesting begins in May. Males take most of the responsibility of raising the young while females start second broods. Only 9 to 12 days separate broods. Feeds on the ground by scratching backward with both feet simultaneously.

winter

breeding

WINTER

GOLDEN-CROWNED SPARROW
Zonotrichia atricapilla

Size: 7" (18 cm)

Male: All-brown sparrow with a heavy body, long tail and yellow spot in the center of a black crown. Gray around head and chest. Upper bill (mandible) is darker than the lower bill (mandible). Winter has varying amounts of black on crown.

Female: same as male

Juvenile: similar to adult, lacks the black and yellow crown

Nest: cup; female and male build; 1 brood a year

Eggs: 3-5; bluish white with brown markings

Incubation: 10-14 days; female incubates

Fledging: 8-14 days; female and male feed young

Migration: complete, to western coastal U.S., Mexico

Food: insects, seeds, berries

Compare: The White-crowned Sparrow (pg. 97) is similar, but lacks the yellow patch in the center of Golden-crowned's black crown.

Stan's Notes: One of the common winter sparrows, often seen in flocks with other sparrows. In the winter there are varying amounts of black on the head, but the yellow patch remains the same. Male feeds the female while she incubates. Nests in western Canada and Alaska, not in Washington.

FOX SPARROW
Passerella iliaca

YEAR-ROUND
MIGRATION
SUMMER
WINTER

Size: 7" (18 cm)

Male: Plump rusty brown sparrow with a heavily streaked, rust-colored breast. Solid rust tail.

Female: same as male

Juvenile: same as adult

Nest: cup; female builds; 2 broods per year

Eggs: 2-4; pale green with reddish markings

Incubation: 12-14 days; female incubates

Fledging: 10-11 days; female and male feed young

Migration: complete, to western coastal U.S., southern states

Food: seeds, insects, comes to feeders

Compare: Rust coloring differentiates it from all other sparrows. Male and female Spotted Towhee (pg. 7) are found in a similar habitat, but the male has a black head and both have white bellies.

Stan's Notes: The winter Fox Sparrows are not the same variety as the resident summer breeders. In winter, northern Pacific varieties (shown), which are a dark brown, displace breeding Slate-colored Fox Sparrows (not shown), which have gray heads and backs. Nests in brush on the ground and along forest edges. Scratches like a chicken with both feet at the same time to find seeds and insects. The name "Sparrow" comes from the Anglo-Saxon word *spearwa*, meaning "flutterer," as applies to any small bird. "Fox" refers to the bird's rusty color.

SWAINSON'S THRUSH
Catharus ustulatus

Size: 7" (18 cm)

Male: Dusty-brown head, back and wings. Brown smudges and spots especially beneath chin and on the chest, and on an off-white belly. A small, thin two-toned bill, yellow under and black above.

Female: same as male

Juvenile: similar to adult, less distinct spots on chest

Nest: cup; female builds; 1 brood per year

Eggs: 3-5; pale blue with brown markings

Incubation: 12-14 days; female incubates

Fledging: 10-14 days; female and male feed young

Migration: complete, to Mexico, Central America and South America

Food: insects, fruit

Compare: Similar shape as American Robin (pg. 211), but is smaller and lacks the red breast.

Stan's Notes: The most common of the thrush species in the state. Found throughout western Washington in lower elevation conifer forests. Often hard to see because most of the time it stays on the ground in thick vegetation. Feeds mostly on insects in spring and summer, adding fruit to its diet in late summer. Nests in shrubs or low in conifer trees, building a bulky cup nest consisting of grass, bark and moss, all glued together with mud.

HORNED LARK
Eremophila alpestris

Size: 7-8" (18-20 cm)

Male: Brown with a slightly orange nape of neck. Black necklace. Yellow chin and forehead. Black spot near eyes, behind black bill. Two tiny "horns" on head can be hard to see.

Female: same as male, only duller, "horns" are even less noticeable

Juvenile: lacks the black markings and yellow chin, doesn't form "horns" until second year

Nest: ground; female builds; 2-3 broods per year

Eggs: 3-4; gray with brown markings

Incubation: 11-12 days; female incubates

Fledging: 9-12 days; female and male feed young

Migration: partial to non-migrator, to southern states, Mexico, Central and South America

Food: seeds, insects

Compare: Smaller than Meadowlark (pg. 305), which shares the black necklace and yellow chin. Look for the black marks in front of eyes.

Stan's Notes: The only true lark native to North America. A year-round resident, but also moves to find food (seasonal movement). Larks are birds of open ground. Common in rural areas, almost always seen in large flocks at country roads. Population increased over the past 100 years due to clearing land for farming. May have up to three broods per year because they get such an early start. Females perform a fluttering distraction display if nest is disturbed. Females can renest about seven days after brood fledges. The name "Lark" comes from the Middle English word *laverock*, or "a lark."

1 year old

YEAR-ROUND
WINTER

CEDAR WAXWING
Bombycilla cedrorum

Size: 7½" (19 cm)

Male: Very sleek-looking gray-to-brown bird with pointed crest, light yellow belly and bandit-like black mask. Tip of tail is bright yellow and the tips of wings look as if they have been dipped in red wax.

Female: same as male

Juvenile: slightly smaller, overall gray, lacks red wing tips, black mask and sleek appearance, has a heavily streaked chest

Nest: cup; female and male build; 1 brood a year, occasionally 2

Eggs: 4-6; pale blue with brown markings

Incubation: 10-12 days; female incubates

Fledging: 14-18 days; female and male feed young

Migration: partial migrator, moves around to find food

Food: cedar cones, fruit, insects

Compare: Nearly identical to its larger, less common cousin, Bohemian Waxwing (not shown).

Stan's Notes: The name is derived from its red wax-like wing tips and preference for eating small blueberry-like cones of the cedar. Mostly seen in flocks, moving from area to area, looking for berries. Wanders in winter to find available food supplies. More often seen in winter only because naked branches reveal its presence. In the summer, before berries are abundant, it feeds on insects. Spends most of its time at the tops of tall trees. Listen for the very high-pitched whistling sounds that it constantly makes. Obtains mask after the first year.

male pg. 3

female

BROWN-HEADED COWBIRD
Molothrus ater

Size: 7½" (19 cm)

Female: Dull brown bird with no obvious markings. Pointed, sharp gray bill.

Male: glossy black bird, chocolate brown head

Juvenile: similar to female, only dull gray color and a streaked chest

Nest: no nest; lays eggs in nests of other birds

Eggs: 5-7; white with brown markings

Incubation: 10-13 days; host bird incubates eggs

Fledging: 10-11 days; host birds feed young

Migration: complete, to southern states

Food: insects, seeds, will come to seed feeders

Compare: Female Red-winged Blackbird (pg. 117) is slightly larger, and has white eyebrows and a streaked breast. European Starling (pg. 5) has speckles and a shorter tail.

Stan's Notes: A member of the blackbird family. Of approximately 750 species of parasitic birds worldwide, this is the only parasitic bird in the state, laying all eggs in host birds' nests, leaving others to raise its young. Cowbirds are known to have laid eggs in nests of over 200 species of birds. Some birds reject cowbird eggs, but most raise them, even to the exclusion of their own young. Look for warblers and other birds feeding young birds twice their own size. At one time cowbirds followed bison to feed on the insects attracted to the animals.

winter

breeding

SPOTTED SANDPIPER
Actitis macularia

Size: 8" (20 cm)

Male: Olive brown back. Long bill and long dull yellow legs. White chest. A white line over the eyes. Breeding adult has black spots on chest. Winter adult lacks breast spots.

Female: same as male

Juvenile: similar to winter adult, with a darker bill

Nest: ground; female and male build; 2 broods per year

Eggs: 3-4; brownish with brown markings

Incubation: 20-24 days; male incubates

Fledging: 17-21 days; male feeds young

Migration: complete, southern states, South America, partial migrator, to western Washington

Food: aquatic insects

Compare: The Killdeer (pg. 125) has two black bands around neck. Look for Spotted Sandpiper to bob its tail up and down while standing. Look for the breeding Spotted Sandpiper's black spots extending from chest down to the abdomen.

Stan's Notes: One of the few shorebirds that will dive underwater if pursued. Able to fly straight up out of the water. Flies with wings held in a cup-like arc, rarely lifting them above a horizontal plane. Constantly bobs its tail while standing and walks as if delicately balanced. Female mates with multiple males and lays eggs in up to five different nests. Male incubates and cares for young. In winter plumage, it lacks spots.

male pg. 255

female

BLACK-HEADED GROSBEAK
Pheucticus melanocephalus

MIGRATION
SUMMER

Size: 8" (20 cm)

Female: Appears like an overgrown sparrow. Overall brown with lighter-colored chest and belly, prominent white eyebrows and a large two-toned bill.

Male: burnt orange chest, neck and rump, black head, tail and wings with irregular-shaped white wing patches, large bill with upper bill darker than lower

Juvenile: similar to adult of the same sex

Nest: cup; female builds; 1 brood per year

Eggs: 3-4; pale green or bluish, brown markings

Incubation: 11-13 days; female and male incubate

Fledging: 11-13 days; female and male feed young

Migration: complete, to Mexico, Central America and South America

Food: insects, seeds, fruit

Compare: Female House Finch (pg. 77) is smaller, has more streaking on the chest and bill isn't as large. Look for female Grosbeak's unusual bicolored bill.

Stan's Notes: A cosmopolitan bird that nests in a wide variety of habitats, seeming to prefer the foothills in the western part of the state slightly more than other places. Both males and females sing, and aggressively defend their nests against intruders. Song is very similar to the American Robin's and Western Tanager's, making it difficult to tell them apart by song. Populations are increasing in Washington and across the U.S.

113

winter
pg. 209

breeding

DUNLIN
Calidris alpina

MIGRATION
WINTER

Size: 8-9" (20-22.5 cm)

Male: Distinctive breeding adult has a rusty red back, finely streaked chest and an obvious black patch on the belly. Stout bill, curving slightly downward at the tip. Black legs.

Female: slightly larger than male, with longer bill

Juvenile: slightly rusty back with spotty chest

Nest: ground; the male and female build; 1 brood per year

Eggs: 2-4; an olive-buff or a blue-green with red-brown markings

Incubation: 21-22 days; male and female incubate, the male during day, female at night

Fledging: 19-21 days; male feeds young, female often leaves before young fledge

Migration: complete, to the coasts of the U.S., Mexico and Central America

Food: insects

Compare: A unique shorebird. Look for the obvious black belly patch and down-curved bill of breeding Dunlin.

Stan's Notes: Breeding plumage more commoly seen in spring. Flights include heights up to 100 feet (30 m) with brief gliding alternating with shallow flutters, and rhythmic, repeating song. Huge flocks fly synchronously, with birds twisting and turning, flashing light and dark undersides. The males tend to fly farther south than females in the winter. Doesn't nest in the state.

female

male pg. 9

RED-WINGED BLACKBIRD
Agelaius phoeniceus

Size: 8½" (22 cm)

Female: Heavily streaked brown bird with a pointed brown bill and white eyebrows.

Male: jet black bird with red and yellow patches on upper wings, pointed black bill

Juvenile: same as female

Nest: cup; female builds; 2-3 broods per year

Eggs: 3-4; bluish green with brown markings

Incubation: 10-12 days; female incubates

Fledging: 11-14 days; female and male feed young

Migration: non-migrator to partial migrator

Food: seeds, insects, will come to seed feeders

Compare: Female Brewer's Blackbird (pg. 119) and female Yellow-headed Blackbird (pg. 123) are larger. Female Brown-headed Cowbird (pg. 109) is smaller. All three species lack white eyebrows and heavily streaked chest of the female Red-winged Blackbird.

Stan's Notes: One of the most widespread and numerous birds in the state. It is a sure sign of spring when the Red-winged Blackbirds return to the marshes. Flocks of up to 100,000 birds have been reported. Males return before the females and defend territories by singing from the tops of surrounding vegetation. Will repeat call from top of cattail while showing off its red and yellow wing bars (epaulets). Nests are usually over shallow water in thick stands of cattails. They feed mostly on seeds in spring and fall, switching to insects during summer. Females choose mate.

117

male pg. 11

female

BREWER'S BLACKBIRD
Euphagus cyanocephalus

YEAR-ROUND
WINTER

Size: 9" (22.5 cm)

Female: An overall grayish brown bird. Legs and bill nearly black. While most have dark eyes, some have yellow or pale eyes.

Male: glossy black, shining green in direct light, head purplish, bright yellow or pale eyes

Juvenile: similar to female

Nest: cup; female builds; 1-2 broods per year

Eggs: 4-6; gray with brown markings

Incubation: 12-14 days; female incubates

Fledging: 13-14 days; female and male feed young

Migration: non-migrator to partial migrator

Food: insects, seeds, fruit

Compare: Larger in size and darker in color than the female Brown headed Cowbird (pg. 109). Female Red-winged Blackbird (pg. 117) is similar in size, but has a heavily streaked chest and prominent white eyebrows.

Stan's Notes: Common blackbird of open areas such as farms, wet pastures, mountain meadows and even desert scrub. Usually nests in a shrub, small tree or directly on the ground. Prefers nesting in small colonies of up to 20 pairs. Will flock with other species such as Red-winged Blackbirds and cowbirds. A common cowbird host.

in flight

COMMON NIGHTHAWK
Chordeiles minor

Size: 9" (22.5 cm)

Male: A camouflaged brown and white bird with white chin. A distinctive white band across wings and the tail, seen only in flight.

Female: similar to male, but with tan chin, lacks the white tail band

Juvenile: similar to female

Nest: no nest; lays eggs on the ground, usually on rocks, or on rooftop

Eggs: 2; cream with lavender markings

Incubation: 19-20 days; female and male incubate

Fledging: 20-21 days; female and male feed young

Migration: complete, to South America

Food: insects caught in air

Compare: Look for the obvious white wing band of Nighthawk in flight, and the characteristic flap-flap-flap-glide flight pattern.

Stan's Notes: Usually only seen flying at dusk or after sunset, but not uncommon for it to be sitting on a fence post sleeping during the day. A very noisy bird, repeating a "peenting" call during flight. Alternates slow wing beats with bursts of quick wing beats. Prolific insect eater. Prefers gravel rooftops for nesting in cities and nests on the ground in country. Male's distinctive springtime mating ritual is a steep diving flight terminated with a loud popping noise. One of the first birds to migrate each fall. Can be more common in cities than in country.

male pg. 13

female

MIGRATION
SUMMER

YELLOW-HEADED BLACKBIRD
Xanthocephalus xanthocephalus

Size: 9-11" (22.5-28 cm)

Female: A large brown bird with a dull yellow head and chest. Slightly smaller than male.

Male: black bird with a lemon-yellow head, chest and nape of neck, black mask and gray bill, white wing patches

Juvenile: similar to female

Nest: cup; female builds; 2 broods per year

Eggs: 3-5; greenish white with brown markings

Incubation: 11-13 days; female incubates

Fledging: 9-12 days; female feeds young

Migration: complete, to southern states and Mexico

Food: insects, seeds

Compare: Larger than female Red-winged Blackbird (pg. 117), which has white eyebrows and streaked chest.

Stan's Notes: Usually heard before seen, Yellow-headed Blackbird has a low, hoarse, raspy or metallic call. Nests in deep water marshes unlike its cousin, the Red-winged Blackbird, which prefers shallow water. The male gives an impressive mating display, flying with head drooped and feet and tail pointing down while steadily beating its wings. The female incubates alone and feeds between three to five young. Young keep low and out of sight for up to three weeks before starting to fly. Migrates in flocks of up to 200 with other blackbirds. Flocks made up mainly of males return first in late March and early April; females return later. Most colonies consist of 20 to 100 nests.

YEAR-ROUND
SUMMER

KILLDEER
Charadrius vociferus

Size: 11" (28 cm)

Male: An upland shorebird with two black bands around the neck like a necklace. A brown back and white belly. Bright reddish-orange rump, visible in flight.

Female: same as male

Juvenile: similar to adult, with only one neck band

Nest: ground; male builds; 2 broods per year

Eggs: 3-5; tan with brown markings

Incubation: 24-28 days; male and female incubate

Fledging: 25 days; male and female lead their young to food

Migration: partial migrator to complete, to southern states, Mexico and Central America

Food: insects

Compare: The Spotted Sandpiper (pg. 111) is found around water and lacks the two neck bands of the Killdeer.

Stan's Notes: The only shorebird with two black neck bands. It is known for its broken wing impression, which draws intruders away from nest. Once clear of the nest, the Killdeer takes flight. Nests are only a slight depression in a gravel area, often very difficult to see. Young look like yellow cotton balls on stilts when first hatched, but quickly molt to appear similar to parents. Able to follow parents and peck for insects soon after birth. Is technically classified as a shorebird, but doesn't live at the shore. Often found in vacant fields or along railroads. Has a very distinctive "kill-jer" call.

male

female

AMERICAN KESTREL
Falco sparverius

Size: 10-12" (25-30 cm)

Male: Rusty brown back and tail. A white breast with dark spots. Double black vertical lines on white face. Blue gray wings. Distinctive wide black band with a white edge on tip of rusty tail.

Female: similar to male, but slightly larger, has rusty brown wings and dark bands on tail

Juvenile: same as adult of the same sex

Nest: cavity; doesn't build a nest within; 1 brood per year

Eggs: 4-5; white with brown markings

Incubation: 29-31 days; male and female incubate

Fledging: 30-31 days; female and male feed young

Migration: non-migrator to partial migrator

Food: insects, small mammals and birds, reptiles

Compare: Similar to other falcons. Look for the two vertical black stripes on face of Kestrel. No other small bird of prey has rusty-colored back or tail.

Stan's Notes: Formerly called Sparrow Hawk due to its small size. Could be called Grasshopper Hawk because it eats many grasshoppers. Hovers near roads before diving for prey. Adapts quickly to a wooden nest box. Has pointed swept-back wings, seen in flight. Perches nearly upright. Kestrels are rare raptors in that males and females have quite different markings. Watch for them to pump their tails up and down after landing on perches.

red-shafted
male

yellow-shafted
female

red-shafted
female

yellow-shafted
male

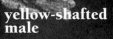

NORTHERN FLICKER
Colaptes auratus

Size: 12" (30 cm)

Male: Brown and black woodpecker with a large white rump patch visible only when flying. Black necklace above speckled breast. Gray head with a brown cap. Red mustache.

Female: same as male, but lacking red mustache

Juvenile: same as adult of the same sex

Nest: cavity; female and male excavate; 1 brood per year

Eggs: 5-8; white without markings

Incubation: 11-14 days; female and male incubate

Fledging: 25-28 days; female and male feed young

Migration: non-migrator in Washington

Food: insects, especially ants and beetles

Compare: Female Williamson's Sapsucker (pg. 31) has a finely barred back with a yellow belly and lacks Flicker's black spots on chest and belly.

Stan's Notes: The flicker is the only woodpecker to regularly feed on the ground, preferring ants and beetles. Produces antacid saliva to neutralize the acidic defense of ants. Male usually selects a nest site, taking up to 12 days to excavate. Some have been successful attracting flickers to nesting boxes stuffed with sawdust. Northern Flickers in western states flash reddish orange under the wings and tails when flying, while those in eastern states have golden yellow wing linings and tails. Both varieties undulate deeply during flight while giving a loud "wacka-wacka" call. Hybrids between western red-shafted and eastern yellow-shafted versions occur in the Great Plains, where their ranges overlap.

YEAR-ROUND

MOURNING DOVE
Zenaida macroura

Size: 12" (30 cm)

Male: Smooth fawn-colored dove with gray patch on the head. Iridescent pink, green around neck. A single black spot behind and below eyes. Black spots on wings and tail. Pointed wedge-shaped tail with white edges.

Female: similar to male, lacking iridescent pink and green neck feathers

Juvenile: spotted and streaked

Nest: platform; female and male build; 2 broods per year

Eggs: 2; white without markings

Incubation: 13-14 days; male and female incubate, the male during day, female at night

Fledging: 12-14 days; female and male feed young

Migration: partial migrator, will move around to find food, or complete, to southern states

Food: seeds, will come to seed feeders

Compare: Lacks the color combinations of Rock Dove (pg. 221). Smaller than Band-tailed Pigeon (pg. 223) and lacks Pigeon's white collar.

Stan's Notes: Name comes from its mournful cooing. Mates for life, roughly seven to ten years. A ground feeder, its head bobs as it walks. One of the few birds to drink without lifting head, same as Rock Dove. Parents feed the young a regurgitated liquid called crop-milk for the first few days of life. Flimsy platform nest of twigs often falls apart in a storm. Wind rushing through wing feathers in flight creates a characteristic whistling sound.

PIED-BILLED GREBE
Podilymbus podiceps

Size: 13" (33 cm)

Male: Small brown water bird with a black chin and black ring around a thick, chicken-like ivory bill. Puffy white patch under the tail.

Female: same as male

Juvenile: paler than adult, with white spots and gray chest, belly and bill

Nest: floating platform; female and male build; 1 brood per year

Eggs: 5-7; bluish white without markings

Incubation: 22-24 days; female and male incubate

Fledging: 22-24 days; female and male feed young

Migration: complete, to southern states, Mexico and Central America, non-migrator in most of Washington

Food: crayfish, aquatic insects, fish

Compare: The smallest brown water bird that dives underwater for long periods of time.

Stan's Notes: A common resident bird. Often seen diving for fish, crayfish and aquatic insects. It slowly sinks like a submarine when disturbed. Formerly called Hell-diver because of the length of time it stays submerged. Can surface far away from where it went under. Builds a platform nest on a floating mat in the water. Particularly sensitive to pollution. Adapted well to life on the water, with short wings, lobed toes and legs set close to the rear of the body. While swimming is easy, it is very awkward on land. The name "Grebe" probably came from the Old English word *krib*, meaning "crest," a reference to the Great Crested Grebe found in Europe.

male pg. 35

female

BUFFLEHEAD
Bucephala albeola

Size: 13-15" (33-38 cm)

Female: Brownish gray duck with dark brown head. White patch on cheek, just behind eyes.

Male: striking black and white duck with a head that shines green purple in sunlight, large white bonnet-like patch on back of head

Juvenile: similar to female

Nest: cavity; female lines old woodpecker cavity; 1 brood per year

Eggs: 8-10; ivory to olive without markings

Incubation: 29-31 days; female incubates

Fledging: 50-55 days; female leads young to food

Migration: complete, to southern states, Mexico and Central America

Food: aquatic insects

Compare: Slightly smaller than female Lesser Scaup (pg. 143), which has a white mark at base of bill, compared with a white patch on the female Bufflehead's cheek.

Stan's Notes: Common diving duck that travels with other ducks. Usually seen during migrations and winter, arriving late in August and remaining in Washington the entire winter. Most commonly found in sheltered bays and coastal harbors, it is also found inland on rivers and lakes. Nests in old woodpecker cavities. Unlike other ducks, young remain in nests for up to two days before venturing out with their mothers. Female is very territorial and remains with the same mate for many years.

male

female

GREEN-WINGED TEAL
Anas crecca

Size: 15" (38 cm)

Male: A chestnut head with a dark green patch behind the eyes extending down to nape of the neck and outlined in white. Gray body with a butter-yellow tail.

Female: light brown with black spots, and a small black bill

Juvenile: same as female

Nest: ground; female builds; 1 brood per year

Eggs: 8-10; creamy white without markings

Incubation: 21-23 days; female incubates

Fledging: 32-34 days; female teaches young to feed

Migration: complete, to western coastal U.S., southern states, non-migrator in Washington

Food: aquatic plants and insects

Compare: Male Green-winged Teal is not as colorful as the male Wood Duck (pg. 243). Female Green-winged Teal is very similar to larger female Cinnamon Teal (pg. 141), which has a larger bill and lacks the dark line through eyes. Female Blue-winged Teal (pg. 139) has a slight white mark near base of bill.

Stan's Notes: One of the smallest dabbling ducks, tipping forward in the water to glean aquatic insects and plants from the bottom of shallow ponds. Will feed in fields but returns to freshwater ponds. Common year-round resident in Washington, breeding in eastern part of the state, spending the winter on the coast. Green speculum most obvious when in flight.

female

male

BLUE-WINGED TEAL
Anas discors

Size: 15-16" (38-40 cm)

Male: Small, plain-looking brown duck speckled with black. A gray head with a large white crescent-shaped mark at base of bill. Black tail with small white patch. Blue wing patch (speculum) usually only seen in flight.

Female: duller version of male, lacks facial crescent mark and white patch on tail, showing only slight white at base of bill

Juvenile: same as female

Nest: ground; female builds; 1 brood per year

Eggs: 8-11; creamy white

Incubation: 23-27 days; female incubates

Fledging: 35-44 days; female feeds young

Migration: complete, to southern states, Mexico and Central America

Food: aquatic plants, seeds, aquatic insects

Compare: Male Blue-winged has a distinct white face marking. The female is nearly half the size of female Mallard (pg. 171) and is similar to female Wood Duck (pg. 149), but lacks Wood Duck's eye ring and crest. The female Cinnamon Teal (pg. 141) has a red tinge.

Stan's Notes: A common duck found mostly on the coast. Known to hybridize with Cinnamon Teals. Nest is built some distance from water. Female will perform distraction display to protect nest and young. Male leaves female near end of incubation. Planting crops and cultivating to pond edges are causing a decline in population.

male

female

CINNAMON TEAL
Anas cyanoptera

Size: 16" (40 cm)

Male: Deep cinnamon head, neck and belly. Light brown back. Dark gray bill. Deep red eyes. Non-breeding (July to September) male is overall brown with a red tinge.

Female: overall brown with a pale brown head, long shovel-like bill, green patch on wings

Juvenile: similar to female

Nest: ground; female builds; 1 brood per year

Eggs: 7-12; pinkish white without markings

Incubation: 21-25 days; female incubates

Fledging: 40-50 days; female teaches young to feed

Migration: partial to complete, to West coast, Mexico

Food: aquatic plants and insects, seeds

Compare: Male Teal shares the cinnamon sides of the larger male Northern Shoveler (pg. 245), but lacks Shoveler's green head and very large spoon-shaped bill. Female Cinnamon Teal looks very similar to the smaller female Green-winged Teal (pg. 137), which has a dark line through the eyes.

Stan's Notes: The most common breeding teal in the state, found in low wetlands on both sides of the Cascades. The male teal is one of the most stunningly beautiful ducks. If threatened, the female will feign a wing injury to lure predators away from young. Prefers to nest along alkaline marshes and shallow lakes, within 75 yards (68 m) of the water. Mallards and other ducks often lay eggs in teal nests, resulting in many nests totaling over 15 eggs.

male pg. 37

female

LESSER SCAUP
Aythya affinis

YEAR-ROUND
MIGRATION
SUMMER
WINTER

Size: 16-17" (40-43 cm)

Female: Overall brown duck with dull white patch at base of light-gray bill. Yellow eyes.

Male: white and gray, the chest and head appear nearly black but head appears purple with green highlights in direct sun, yellow eyes

Juvenile: same as female

Nest: ground; female builds; 1 brood per year

Eggs: 8-14; olive buff without markings

Incubation: 22-28 days; female incubates

Fledging: 45-50 days; female teaches young to feed

Migration: complete, to western coastal U.S., southern states, Mexico, Central America, northern South America

Food: aquatic plants and insects

Compare: Smaller than female Wood Duck (pg. 149), which has white around the eyes, but lacks the white mark at base of bill. Look for the white patch at base of bill to help identify the female Lesser Scaup.

Stan's Notes: Common diving duck, completely submerging itself to feed on the bottom of lakes, unlike dabbling ducks which only tip forward to reach the bottom. Frequently seen in large flocks numbering in the thousands on area lakes and ponds, and along the coast in winter. When seen in flight, note the bold white stripe under the wings. A rare breeder in Washington, breeding north of the state through Alaska. Interesting baby-sitting arrangement in which the young form groups tended by one to three adult females.

male pg. 39

female

HOODED MERGANSER
Lophodytes cucullatus

Size: 16-19" (40-48 cm)

Female: Sleek brown and rust bird with a red head. Ragged "hair" on back of head. Long, thin brown bill.

Male: same size and shape as female, but black back and rust sides, crest "hood" raises to reveal large white patch, long black bill

Juvenile: similar to female

Nest: cavity; female lines old woodpecker hole; 1 brood per year

Eggs: 10-12; white without markings

Incubation: 32-33 days; female incubates

Fledging: 71 days; female feeds young

Migration: complete, to western coastal U.S., Mexico

Food: small fish, aquatic insects

Compare: Smaller than female Common Merganser (pg. 267), which has a white chin and a large orange bill. Larger than female Lesser Scaup (pg. 143), which has a dull white patch at base of bill.

Stan's Notes: A small diving bird of shallow-water ponds, sloughs, lakes and rivers. Rarely found away from wooded areas, where it nests in natural cavities or nest boxes. The female will "dump" eggs into other female Hooded Merganser nests, resulting in 20 to 25 eggs in some nests. The male Hooded Merganser can voluntarily raise and lower its crest to show off the large white patch on its head. Mergansers have been known to share a nesting cavity with Wood Ducks sitting side by side.

RUFFED GROUSE
Bonasa umbellus

Size: 16-19" (40-48 cm)

Male: Brown chicken-like bird with long squared tail. Wide black band near tip of tail. Is able to fan tail like a turkey. Tuft of feathers on the head stands like a crown. Black ruffs on sides of neck.

Female: same as male

Juvenile: same as adult

Nest: ground; female builds; 1 brood per year

Eggs: 9-12; tan with light brown markings

Incubation: 23-24 days; female incubates

Fledging: 10-12 days; female leads young to food

Migration: non-migrator

Food: seeds, insects, fruit, leaf buds

Compare: Ring-necked Pheasant (pg. 173) is larger, with iridescent feathers and a long pointed tail. Look for a feathered tuft on the head and black neck ruffs.

Stan's Notes: A common bird of deep woods. Often seen in aspen or other trees, feeding on leaf buds. In the more northern climates, grows bristles on its feet during the winter to serve as snowshoes. When there is enough snow, it will dive into a snowbank to roost at night. In spring, male raises crest, fans tail feathers, and stands on logs and drums with wings to attract females. Drumming sound comes from cupped wings moving air, not pounding on chest or log. Female will perform distraction display to protect young. Two color morphs, red and gray, most apparent in the tail. Black ruffs around the neck gave rise to its common name.

male pg. 243

female

WOOD DUCK
Aix sponsa

Size: 17-20" (43-50 cm)

Female: A small brown dabbling duck. Bright white eye ring and a not-so-obvious crest. A blue patch on wing is often hidden.

Male: highly ornamented with a green head and crest patterned with white and black, rusty chest, white belly and red eyes

Juvenile: same as female

Nest: cavity; female lines old woodpecker cavity; 1 brood per year

Eggs: 10-15; creamy white without markings

Incubation: 28-36 days; female incubates

Fledging: 56-68 days; female teaches young to feed

Migration: complete, to southern states, partial to non-migrator in Washington

Food: aquatic insects, plants, seeds

Compare: Smaller than the female Mallard (pg. 171) and similar to the female Blue-winged Teal (pg. 139). Mallard and Teal lack the female Duck's bright white eye ring and crest.

Stan's Notes: A common duck of quiet, shallow backwater ponds. Nests in old woodpecker holes or in nest boxes. Often seen flying deep in forest or perched high on tree branches. Female takes flight with loud squealing call and enters nest cavity from full flight. Will lay eggs in a neighboring female nest (egg dumping), resulting in some clutches in excess of 20 eggs. Young stay in nest cavity only 24 hours after hatching, then jump from up to 30 feet (9 m) to the ground or water to follow their mother, never returning to the nest.

male

female

AMERICAN WIGEON
Anas americana

Size: 19" (48 cm)

Male: A brown duck with a rounded head, a long pointed tail and short, black-tipped grayish bill. Obvious white cap. Deep green patch starting behind eyes, streaking down neck. White belly and wing linings, seen in flight. Non-breeding lacks white cap, green patch.

Female: light brown with a pale gray head, a short, black-tipped grayish bill, green wing patch (speculum), dark eye spot, white belly and wing linings, seen in flight

Juvenile: similar to female

Nest: ground; female builds; 1 brood per year

Eggs: 7-12; white without markings

Incubation: 23-25 days; female incubates

Fledging: 37-48 days; female teaches young to feed

Migration: partial migrator to non-migrator, along the West coast from Alaska to Mexico

Food: aquatic plants, seeds

Compare: The male Wigeon is easily identified by the white cap. Female Wigeon is similar to the female Cinnamon Teal (pg. 141), but has a short black-tipped bill and is less common.

Stan's Notes: Often in small flocks or with other ducks. Prefers shallow lakes. Male stays with female the first week of incubation only. Female raises young. If threatened, female feigns injury while young run and hide. Conceals upland nest in tall vegetation within 50 to 250 yards (46 to 228 m) of water. Winters on the West coast.

male pg. 245

female

NORTHERN SHOVELER
Anas clypeata

YEAR-ROUND
SUMMER

Size: 20" (50 cm)

Female: Medium-sized brown duck speckled with black. Blue wing patch. An extraordinarily large spoon-shaped bill, almost always held pointed toward the water.

Male: same spoon-shaped bill, iridescent green head, rusty sides and white breast

Juvenile: same as female

Nest: ground; female builds; 1 brood per year

Eggs: 9-12; olive without markings

Incubation: 22-25 days; female incubates

Fledging: 30-60 days; female leads young to food

Migration: complete, southern states, Mexico, Central America, non-migrator in Washington

Food: aquatic insects, plants

Compare: Similar color as female Mallard (pg. 171), but Mallard lacks the Shoveler's large bill. Larger than female Wood Duck (pg. 149) and lacks the white eye ring. Look for the female Shoveler's large spoon-shaped bill to help identify.

Stan's Notes: One of several species of shoveler, so called because of the peculiarly shaped bill. The Northern Shoveler is the only species of these ducks in North America. Seen in small flocks of five to ten, swimming low in water with large bills always pointed toward the water, as if they're too heavy to lift. Feeds primarily by filtering tiny plants and insects from the water's surface with bill.

female

male pg. 227

GADWALL
Anas strepera

Size: 20" (50 cm)

Female: Very similar to the female Mallard. Mottled brown with pronounced color change from dark brown body to light brown neck and head. Wing linings are bright white, seen in flight. Small white wing patch, seen when swimming. Gray bill with orange sides.

Male: plump gray duck with a brown head and distinctive black rump, white belly, bright white wing linings, small white wing patch, chestnut-tinged wings, gray bill

Juvenile: similar to female

Nest: ground; lined with fine grass, and down feathers plucked from mother's breast; 1 brood per year

Eggs: 8-11; white without markings

Incubation: 24-27 days; female incubates

Fledging: 48-56 days; young feed themselves

Migration: complete, southern states, central Mexico, non-migrator in Washington

Food: aquatic insects

Compare: The female Gadwall is very similar to female Mallard (pg. 171). Look for Gadwall's white wing patch and gray bill with orange sides.

Stan's Notes: A duck of shallow marshes with lots of vegetation. Found in freshwater wetlands in eastern Washington, but is most common in the southern part of Puget Sound. Nests on land within 300 feet (100 m) of water. Establishes pair bond during winter.

soaring light morph

intermediate morph

light morph

dark morph

soaring dark morph

MIGRATION
SUMMER

SWAINSON'S HAWK
Buteo swainsoni

Size: 21" (53 cm); up to 4½-foot wingspan

Male: Highly variable-plumaged hawk with three easily distinguishable color morphs. Light morph is brown with a white belly, a warm rusty breast and a white face. Intermediate has a dark breast, rusty belly and white at the base of the bill. Dark morph is nearly all dark brown with a rusty color low on belly.

Female: same as male

Juvenile: similar to adult

Nest: platform; female and male build; 1 brood per year

Eggs: 2-4; bluish or white, some brown markings

Incubation: 28-35 days; female and male incubate

Fledging: 28-30 days; female and male feed young

Migration: complete, to Central and South America

Food: small mammals, insects, snakes, birds

Compare: The Red-tailed Hawk (pg. 159) has a white chest with brown belly band. Similar size as Rough-legged Hawk (pg. 161), but Rough-legged has a lighter trailing edge of wings.

Stan's Notes: Slender open country hawk that hunts mammals, insects, snakes and birds when soaring (kiting) or perching. Often flies with slightly upturned wings in a teetering, vulture-like flight. The light morph is the most common of the three color types, with intermediate and dark also common. Even minor nest disturbance can cause nest failure. Often gathers in large flocks to migrate.

soaring

RED-TAILED HAWK
Buteo jamaicensis

YEAR-ROUND

Size: 19-25" (48-63 cm); up to 4-foot wingspan

Male: Large hawk with amazing variety of colors from bird to bird, from chocolate brown to nearly all white. Often brown with a white breast and a distinctive brown belly band. Rust red tail usually only seen from above. Underside of wing is white with small dark patch on leading edge near shoulder.

Female: same as male, often larger

Juvenile: similar to adults, lacking the red tail, has a speckled chest

Nest: platform; male and female build; 1 brood per year

Eggs: 2-3; white, without markings or sometimes marked with brown

Incubation: 30-35 days; female and male incubate

Fledging: 45-46 days; male and female feed young

Migration: non-migrator to partial migrator

Food: mice, birds, snakes, insects

Compare: Swainson's Hawk (pg. 157) is slimmer with longer, more pointed wings and longer tail.

Stan's Notes: A common hawk of open country and cities in the state, often seen perched on freeway light posts. Look for it circling above open fields, searching for prey. Their large stick nests are commonly seen along roads in large trees. Stick nests are lined with finer material such as evergreen needles. Will return to the same nest site each year. Doesn't develop red tail until second year.

dark morph

soaring dark morph

light morph

soaring light morph

ROUGH-LEGGED HAWK
Buteo lagopus

Size: 22" (56 cm); up to 4½-foot wingspan

Male: A hawk of several plumages. All plumages have a long tail with a dark band or bands. Distinctive dark wrists and belly. Relatively long wings, small bill and feet. Light morph has nearly pure white undersides of wings and base of tail. Dark morph is nearly all brown with light gray trailing edge of wings.

Female: same as male, only larger

Juvenile: same as adults

Nest: platform, on edge of cliff; female and male build; 1 brood per year

Eggs: 2-6; white without markings

Incubation: 28-31 days; female and male incubate

Fledging: 39-43 days; female and male feed young

Migration: complete, to the northern half of the U.S.

Food: small animals, snakes, large insects

Compare: Similar size as Swainson's Hawk (pg. 157), which has narrow pointed wings, as seen in flight, and a lighter leading edge of wings, unlike Rough-legged's lighter trailing edge of wings.

Stan's Notes: Two color morphs, light and dark, light being more common. Common winter resident, nesting in Canada's Northwest Territories and Alaska. More numerous in some years than others. Much smaller and weaker feet than the other birds of prey, which means it must hunt smaller prey. Hunts from the air, usually hovering before diving for small rodents such as mice and voles.

BARRED OWL
Strix varia

Size: 20-24" (50-60 cm)

Male: A chunky brown and gray owl with a large head and dark brown eyes. Dark horizontal barring on chest, and vertical streaking on the belly.

Female: same as male, only slightly larger

Juvenile: same as adults

Nest: cavity; no nesting material is brought in; 1 brood per year

Eggs: 2-3; white without markings

Incubation: 28-33 days; female incubates

Fledging: 42-44 days; female and male feed young

Migration: non-migrator

Food: mammals, small birds

Compare: Lacks the "horns" of the Great Horned Owl (pg. 165) and ear tufts of the tiny Western Screech-Owl (pg. 207). Western Screech-Owl is less than half the size of Barred Owl.

Stan's Notes: A very common owl that can often be seen hunting during the day. Prefers dense woodland with sparse undergrowth. Can be attracted with a simple nest box that has a large opening, which is attached to a tree. The young will stay with the parents for up to four months after fledging. Often sounds like a dog barking just before giving an eight-hoot call that sounds like, "Who-cooks-for-you? Who-cooks-for-you?" The Great Horned Owl sounds like, "Hoo-hoo-hoo-hoooo!"

GREAT HORNED OWL
Bubo virginianus

YEAR-ROUND

Size: 20-25" (50-63 cm)

Male: A robust brown "horned" owl with bright yellow eyes and V-shaped white bib.

Female: same as male, only slightly larger

Juvenile: similar to adults

Nest: no nest; takes over the nests of crows, Great Blue Herons and hawks, or will use partial cavities; 1 brood per year

Eggs: 2; white without markings

Incubation: 26-30 days; female incubates

Fledging: 30-35 days; male and female feed young

Migration: non-migrator

Food: small mammals, birds, snakes, insects

Compare: Barred Owl (pg. 163) has dark eyes and no "horns." Great Horned Owl is more than twice the size of its cousin, the Western Screech-Owl (pg. 207).

Stan's Notes: One of the earliest nesting birds in the state, laying eggs in January and February. Has excellent hearing; able to hear a mouse moving beneath a foot of snow. "Ears" are actually tufts of feathers (horns) and have nothing to do with hearing. Not able to turn head all the way around. Wing feathers are ragged on the end, resulting in a silent flight. The eyelids close from the top down, like humans. Fearless, it is one of the few animals that will kill skunks and porcupines. Because of this, it is sometimes called Flying Tiger.

LONG-BILLED CURLEW
Numenius americanus

Size: 23" (58 cm), including bill

Male: Cinnamon brown with an extremely long, down-curved bill. Long bluish legs. Darker cinnamon wing linings, seen in flight.

Female: same as male, but with a longer bill

Juvenile: same as adults, but with a shorter bill

Nest: ground; female builds; 1 brood per year

Eggs: 5-7; olive green with brown markings

Incubation: 27-30 days; female and male incubate, the female during day, male at night

Fledging: 32-45 days; female and male feed young

Migration: complete, to West coast states, Central and South American coasts

Food: insects, worms, crabs, eggs

Compare: Spotted Sandpiper (pg. 111) is smaller, less than half the size of the Long-billed Curlew. Hard to mistake the exceptionally long bill.

Stan's Notes: The largest of shorebirds, with an appropriate name. The extremely long bill is greater than half the length of its body. Females have longer bills than the males. Juveniles have short bills, which grow into long bills during the first six months. Uses its bill to probe deep into mud for insects and worms. Females incubate during the day, males during the night. Although a shorebird, it is often in grass fields away from the shore. Breeds in open valleys and flatland. Arrives in Washington in April to begin nesting. Will fly as far as 6 miles (10 km) from nest site to find food.

167

male pg. 229

female

NORTHERN HARRIER
Circus cyaneus

YEAR-ROUND
WINTER

Size: 24" (60 cm)

Female: A slim, low-flying hawk. Dark brown back with brown-streaked breast and belly. Large white rump patch and narrow black bands across tail. Tips of wings black.

Male: silver gray with large white rump patch and white belly, faint narrow bands across tail, tips of wings black

Juvenile: similar to female, with an orange breast

Nest: platform; female and male build; 1 brood per year

Eggs: 4-8; bluish white without markings

Incubation: 31-32 days; female incubates

Fledging: 30-35 days; male and female feed young

Migration: partial to non-migrator, to western coastal U.S., southern states, Mexico and Central America

Food: mice, snakes

Compare: Slimmer than Red-tailed Hawk (pg. 159). Look for black bands on tail and a white rump patch.

Stan's Notes: One of the easiest hawks to identify. Harriers glide just above the ground, following the contours of the land while searching for prey. Wings are held just above the horizontal position, tilting back and forth in the wind, similar to Turkey Vultures. Was formerly called Marsh Hawk due to its habit of hunting over marshes. Nests on the ground. At all ages, the Northern Harrier has distinctive owl-like face disks.

male pg. 249

female

MALLARD
Anas platyrhynchos

YEAR-ROUND

Size:	27-28" (69-71 cm)
Female:	All brown with orange and black bill. Small blue and white wing mark (speculum).
Male:	large, bulbous green head, white necklace, rust brown or chestnut chest, combination of gray and white on sides, yellow bill, legs and feet
Juvenile:	same as female, but with a yellow bill
Nest:	ground; female builds; 1 brood per year
Eggs:	7-10; greenish to whitish, unmarked
Incubation:	26-30 days; female incubates
Fledging:	42-52 days; female leads young to food
Migration:	partial to non-migrator in Washington
Food:	seeds, plants, aquatic insects, will come to ground feeders offering corn
Compare:	Female Gadwall (pg. 155) has a gray bill with orange sides, unlike female Mallard's orange and black bill. The female Northern Shoveler (pg. 153) is smaller, with a large spoon-shaped bill. The female Wood Duck (pg. 149) is smaller, with a white eye ring.

Stan's Notes: A familiar duck of lakes and ponds. Will return to place of birth. The name "Mallard" comes from the Latin *masculus*, meaning "male," referring to the habit of males not taking part in raising ducklings. Both male and female have white tails and white underwings. Black central tail feathers of male curl upward.

male

female

RING-NECKED PHEASANT
Phasianus colchicus

YEAR-ROUND

Size: 30-36" (76-90 cm), male, including tail
21-25" (53-63 cm), female, including tail

Male: Golden brown body with a long tail. White ring around neck with purple, green, blue and red head.

Female: smaller, less flamboyant all-brown bird with a long tail

Juvenile: similar to female, with a shorter tail

Nest: ground; female builds; 1 brood per year

Eggs: 8-10; olive brown without markings

Incubation: 23-25 days; female incubates

Fledging: 11-12 days; female leads young to food

Migration: non-migrator

Food: insects, seeds, fruit, visits ground feeders

Compare: Much larger than California Quail (pg. 213) and lacks the teardrop plume on forehead. Ring-necked Pheasant has a long tail, and the male is brightly colored.

Stan's Notes: Introduced from China in the late 1800s. Common now across the U.S. Like many other game birds, their numbers vary greatly, making them common some years and scarce others. The name "Ring-necked" refers to the thin white ring around the male's neck. The name "Pheasant" comes from the Greek word *phaisianos*, meaning "a bird of the River Phasis," which is now known as the River Rioni, located in Europe. Listen for the male's cackling call to attract females.

soaring

juvenile

GOLDEN EAGLE
Aquila chrysaetos

YEAR-ROUND
WINTER

Size: 30-40" (76-102 cm); up to 7-foot wingspan

Male: Uniform dark brown with golden head and nape of neck. Yellow around the base of bill and yellow feet.

Female: same as male

Juvenile: similar to adult, but has white wrist patches and white base of tail

Nest: platform, on cliff; female and male build; 1 brood per year

Eggs: 2; white with brown markings

Incubation: 43-45 days; female and male incubate

Fledging: 66-75 days; female and male feed young

Migration: non-migrator to partial migrator

Food: mammals, birds, reptiles, insects

Compare: Similar to Bald Eagle (pg. 51), lacking the white head and tail. Juvenile Golden Eagle, with its white wrist marks and white base of tail, is often confused with the juvenile Bald Eagle.

Stan's Notes: Large and powerful bird of prey that has no trouble taking larger prey such as jack rabbits. Hunts by perching or soaring and watching for movement. Inhabits mountainous terrain, requiring large territories to provide large supply of food. Thought to mate for life, renewing pair bond late in winter with spectacular high-flying courtship displays. Usually nests on cliff faces, rarely in trees. Uses well-established nest that has been used for generations. Not uncommon for it to add things to nest such as antlers, bones and barbed wire.

WILD TURKEY
Meleagris gallopavo

Size: 36-48" (90-120 cm)

Male: Large, plump brown and bronze bird with striking blue and red bare head. Fan tail and long, straight black beard in center of chest. Spurs on legs.

Female: thinner and less striking than male, usually lacking breast beard

Juvenile: same as adult of the same sex

Nest: ground; female builds; 1 brood per year

Eggs: 10-12; buff white with dull brown markings

Incubation: 27-28 days; female incubates

Fledging: 6-10 days; female leads young to food

Migration: non-migrator

Food: insects, seeds, fruit

Compare: This bird is quite distinctive and unlikely to be confused with others.

Stan's Notes: The largest game bird in the state, and the bird from which the domestic turkey was bred. Almost became our national bird, but lost by one vote to the Bald Eagle. Not a native bird to the state; was introduced to Washington as a game species. Introduced to the western coastal U.S. by as long ago as 1877, though not all were successful. Strong fliers, they can approach 60 miles (97 km) per hour. Able to fly straight up, then away. Eyesight is three times better than humans. Hearing is also excellent; can hear competing males up to a mile away. Males hold "harems" of up to 20 females. Males are known as toms, females are hens and young are called poults. At night, they roost in trees.

juvenile

breeding

chick-feeding adult

MIGRATION

BROWN PELICAN
Pelecanus occidentalis

Size: 48" (120 cm); up to 9-foot wingspan

Male: Gray brown body, black belly, exceptionally long gray bill. Breeding adult has white or yellow head with dark chestnut hind neck. Bright red expandable throat pouch. Adult that is feeding chicks (chick-feeding adult) has a speckled white head. A non-breeding adult has a white head and neck.

Female: similar to male

Juvenile: brown with white breast and belly, does not acquire adult plumage until third year

Nest: platform; female and male build; 1 brood per year

Eggs: 2-4; white without markings

Incubation: 28-30 days; female and male incubate

Fledging: 71-86 days; female and male feed young

Migration: complete, to southern California, Mexico

Food: fish

Compare: An unmistakable bird in Washington.

Stan's Notes: A coastal bird of Washington now, it was recently an endangered species. Having suffered from eggshell thinning during the 1970s due to DDT and other pesticides, it's now reestablishing along the West, East and Gulf coasts. Captures fish by diving head-first into the ocean, opening its large bill and "netting" fish with its gular pouch. Often seen sitting on posts at marinas. Nests in large colonies. Doesn't breed before age 3, when it obtains its breeding plumage. The Pacific variety (shown) has a bright red throat pouch unlike the brown throat patch of the Atlantic and Gulf coast birds.

RUBY-CROWNED KINGLET
Regulus calendula

YEAR-ROUND
MIGRATION
SUMMER
WINTER

Size: 4" (10 cm)

Male: Small, teardrop-shaped green-to-gray bird. Two white wing bars. Hidden ruby-colored crown. White eye ring.

Female: same as male, but lacks ruby crown

Juvenile: same as female

Nest: pendulous; female builds; 1 brood per year

Eggs: 4-5; white with brown markings

Incubation: 11-12 days; female incubates

Fledging: 11-12 days; female and male feed young

Migration: complete, southern states, Mexico, Central America, partial migrator in Washington

Food: insects, berries

Compare: Similar to the Golden-crowned Kinglet (pg. 183), but crown is ruby-colored. The female American Goldfinch (pg. 287) is larger, but shares the olive color and clear breast. Look for the Kinglet's white eye ring.

Stan's Notes: One of the smaller birds in the state, it takes a quick eye to see the male's ruby crown. Most commonly seen during the spring and autumn migrations, look for it flitting around thick shrubs low to the ground. Builds an unusual pendulous (sac-like) nest, intricately woven and decorated on the outside with colored lichens and mosses stuck together with spider webs. The nest is suspended from a branch overlapped by leaves, usually hung high in a mature tree. The name "Kinglet" comes from the Anglo-Saxon *cyning*, or "king," referring to its ruby crown, and the diminutive suffix "let," meaning "small."

YEAR-ROUND
WINTER

GOLDEN-CROWNED KINGLET
Regulus satrapa

Size: 4" (10 cm)

Male: Tiny, plump green-to-gray bird. Distinctive yellow and orange patch with black border on the crown. A white eyebrow mark. Two white wing bars.

Female: same as male, but has a yellow crown with black border, lacks any orange

Juvenile: same as adults, but lacks gold on crown

Nest: pendulous; female builds; 1-2 broods a year

Eggs: 5-9; white or creamy with brown markings

Incubation: 14-15 days; female incubates

Fledging: 14-19 days; female and male feed young

Migration: complete, southern states, Mexico, Central America, non-migrator in Washington

Food: insects, fruit, tree sap

Compare: Similar to Ruby-crowned Kinglet (pg. 181), but Golden-crowned has an obvious crown. Smaller than the female American Goldfinch (pg. 287), which lacks any crown marking.

Stan's Notes: Common year-round resident in the state, but might be more frequently seen during migration when flocks from farther north move through Washington. Often seen in flocks that include chickadees, nuthatches, woodpeckers, Brown Creepers and Ruby-crowned Kinglets. Habit of flicking its wings when moving around. Unusual hanging nest is often made of moss, lichens and spider webs, and lined with bark and feathers. Can have so many eggs in its small nest that eggs are in two layers. Drinks tree sap and feeds by gleaning insects from trees. Can be very tame and approachable.

PYGMY NUTHATCH
Sitta pygmaea

Size: 4¼" (10.5 cm)

Male: Tiny gray-blue black bird with gray-brown crown. Creamy chest with a lighter chin. A relatively short tail, large head and long bill.

Female: same as male

Juvenile: same as adult

Nest: cavity; the female and male build; 1 brood per year

Eggs: 4-8; white with brown markings

Incubation: 14-16 days; female incubates

Fledging: 20-22 days; female and male feed young

Migration: non-migrator

Food: insects, berries, seeds, will visit seed feeders

Compare: Smaller than the Red-breasted Nuthatch (pg. 187) and the White-breasted Nuthatch (pg. 197). The Red-breasted has a rusty red chest, compared with the creamy breast of the Pygmy. White-breasted has a distinctive black cap and a white chest.

Stan's Notes: A bird of Ponderosa Pine forest along the eastern side of the Cascades. Unlike the White-breasted Nuthatch, Pygmy Nuthatches need mature ponderosas with old or decaying wood. Usually drills its own nest cavity. While it doesn't migrate, it forms winter flocks with other birds, such as chickadees and creepers, moving around in search of food. Usually feeds in the crown of a tree or at ends of twigs and branches, where it searches for insects and seeds, unlike the White-breasted or Red-breasted Nuthatches, which usually search trunks of trees for food.

RED-BREASTED NUTHATCH
Sitta canadensis

YEAR-ROUND
WINTER

Size: 4½" (11 cm)

Male: A small gray-backed bird with a black cap and a prominent eye line. A rust red breast and belly.

Female: gray cap, pale undersides

Juvenile: same as female

Nest: cavity; female builds; 1 brood per year

Eggs: 5-6; white with red brown markings

Incubation: 11-12 days; female incubates

Fledging: 14-20 days; female and male feed young

Migration: non-migrator to irruptive, moves around the state in search of food

Food: insects, seeds, visits seed and suet feeders

Compare: Slightly larger than the Pygmy Nuthatch (pg. 185) and smaller than White-breasted Nuthatch (pg. 197), neither of which has the rich red breast of the Red-breasted.

Stan's Notes: Red-breasted Nuthatch behaves like White-breasted and Pygmy Nuthatches, climbing down trunks of trees headfirst. Similar to chickadees, visits seed feeders, quickly grabbing a seed and flying off to crack it open. Will wedge a seed into a crevice and pound it open with several sharp blows. The name "Nuthatch" comes from the Middle English moniker *nuthak*, referring to the bird's habit of wedging a seed into a crevice and hacking it open. Look for it in mature conifers, where it frequently extracts seeds from cones. Doesn't excavate a cavity as a chickadee might; rather, it takes over a former woodpecker or chickadee cavity.

YEAR-ROUND

BUSHTIT
Psaltriparus minimus

Size: 4½" (11 cm)

Male: A dull gray bird with a slightly brown cap. Relatively long tail. Black eyes and legs, and a tiny black bill.

Female: same as male, but has yellow eyes

Juvenile: similar to adults, with dark brown eyes

Nest: pendulous; the female and male build; 1-2 broods per year

Eggs: 5-7; white without markings

Incubation: 10-12 days; female and male incubate

Fledging: 14-15 days; female and male feed young

Migration: non-migrator

Food: insects, seeds, fruit, comes to seed feeders

Compare: Smaller than Black capped, Mountain and Chestnut-backed Chickadees (pp. 191, 193 and 69, respectively), and lacking the black caps and white on faces of the Chickadees.

Stan's Notes: A lively bird, often seen in extended family flocks of up to 20 individuals in open woods and low woodland. Often seen with other species of birds such as kinglets, wrens and chickadees. Easily picked out by its small size, long tail and the extremely short bill. Groups will roost together, huddling tightly to keep warm and save energy. Eyes are pale yellow in adult females, dark brown in juveniles and black in adult males. Away from the coast, adults lack the brown cap, appearing all dull gray.

YEAR-ROUND

BLACK-CAPPED CHICKADEE
Poecile atricapilla

Size: 5" (13 cm)

Male: Familiar gray bird with black cap and throat patch. White chest. Tan belly. Small white wing marks.

Female: same as male

Juvenile: same as adult

Nest: cavity; female and male build or excavate; 1 brood per year

Eggs: 5-7; white with fine brown markings

Incubation: 11-13 days; female and male incubate

Fledging: 14-18 days; female and male feed young

Migration: non-migrator

Food: insects, seeds, fruit, will visit seed and suet feeders

Compare: Similar to Mountain and Chestnut-backed Chickadees (pp. 193 and 69, respectively). Mountain Chickadee has white eyebrows, and the Chestnut-backed has a distinctive chestnut-colored back. Larger than Bushtit (pg. 189), which lacks the Black-capped's black cap and white on face.

Stan's Notes: A common backyard bird that can be attracted with a simple nest box. Makes nest mostly with green moss and lines it with animal fur. Usually the first bird to find a new bird feeder. Can be easily tamed and hand fed. Needs to feed every day during the winter; consequently seen foraging for food during even the worst winter storms. Can have different calls in various regions.

YEAR-ROUND

MOUNTAIN CHICKADEE
Poecile gambeli

Size: 5½" (14 cm)

Male: Overall gray with a black cap, chin and line through the eyes. White eyebrows.

Female: same as male

Juvenile: similar to adult

Nest: cavity, old woodpecker hole or excavates its own; female and male build; 1-2 broods per year

Eggs: 5-8; white without markings

Incubation: 11-14 days; female and male incubate

Fledging: 18-21 days; female and male feed young

Migration: partial migrator

Food: seeds, insects, visits seed and suet feeders

Compare: The Black-capped Chickadee (pg. 191) is similar, but lacks the white eyebrows of the Mountain Chickadee. Larger than Bushtit (pg. 189), which lacks the black cap and white on face.

Stan's Notes: An abundant bird in the state, but more common in northeastern Washington's conifer forest, preferring old growth fir, spruce and Lodgepole Pine forest. Feeds heavily on conifer seeds, and insects. Usually doesn't mingle with Black-capped Chickadees, but does flock with other birds in winter. Moves to lower elevations during winter, returning to high elevations for nesting. Nests in a cavity that it excavates or uses an old woodpecker hole. Will use a nest box. Occasionally uses the same nest site year after year. Lines its nest with moss, hair and feathers. Female won't leave the nest if disturbed, but will hiss and flutter wings.

female pg. 85

male

gray-headed

Oregon male

DARK-EYED JUNCO
Junco hyemalis

Size: 5½" (14 cm)

Male: A round, dark-eyed bird with slate-gray-to-charcoal chest, head and back. White belly. Pink bill. Since the outermost tail feathers are white, tail appears as a white V in flight.

Female: same as male, only tan-to-brown color

Juvenile: similar to female, but has a streaked breast and head

Nest: cup; female and male build; 2 broods a year

Eggs: 3-5; white with reddish brown markings

Incubation: 12-13 days; female incubates

Fledging: 10-13 days; male and female feed young

Migration: partial migrator to non-migrator

Food: seeds, insects, will come to seed feeders

Compare: Rarely confused with any other bird. Large flocks come to feed under bird feeders.

Stan's Notes: Several junco species have now been combined into one, simply called Dark-eyed Junco (see inset photos). A common and widespread nester in forested areas of the state. Very common in most cities during winter, rare during nesting season. Nests in a wide variety of wooded habitats in April and May. Usually seen on the ground in small flocks. It adheres to a rigid social hierarchy, with dominant birds chasing the less dominant birds. Look for its white outer tail feathers flashing in flight. Most comfortable on the ground, juncos will "double-scratch" with both feet to expose seeds and insects. Consumes many weed seeds.

YEAR-ROUND

WHITE-BREASTED NUTHATCH
Sitta carolinensis

Size: 5-6" (13-15 cm)

Male: Slate gray bird with a white belly, black cap and neck. Long thin bill, slightly upturned. Chestnut-colored undertail.

Female: similar to male, gray cap and neck

Juvenile: similar to female

Nest: cavity; the female and male build; 1 brood per year

Eggs: 5-7; white with brown markings

Incubation: 11-12 days; female incubates

Fledging: 13-14 days; female and male feed young

Migration: non-migrator

Food: insects, seeds, visits seed and suet feeders

Compare: Red-breasted Nuthatch (pg. 187) is smaller, with a rusty belly and distinctive black eye line. Pygmy Nuthatch (pg. 185) is smaller and lacks the White-breasted's black cap.

Stan's Notes: The nuthatch's habit of hopping headfirst down tree trunks helps it see insects and insect eggs that birds climbing up the trunk might miss. Incredible climbing agility comes from an extra-long hind toe claw or nail, nearly twice the size of the front toe claws. The name "Nuthatch" comes from the Middle English moniker *nuthak*, referring to the bird's habit of wedging a seed into a crevice and hacking it open. Often seen in mixed flocks of Brown Creepers, chickadees and Downy Woodpeckers. Mated pairs stay together all year, defending small territories. Listen for its characteristic springtime call, "whi-whi-whi-whi," given in February and March. One of 17 worldwide nuthatch species.

male

female

YELLOW-RUMPED WARBLER
Dendroica coronata

YEAR-ROUND
MIGRATION
SUMMER

Size: 5-6" (13-15 cm)

Male: Slate gray bird with black mask and breast. Yellow patch on the head, flanks and rump. White chin and belly. Two white wing bars.

Female: similar to male, duller color, mostly brown and white with matching yellow patches

Juvenile: similar to female

Nest: cup; female builds; 2 broods per year

Eggs: 4-5; white with brown markings

Incubation: 12-13 days; female incubates

Fledging: 10-12 days; female and male feed young

Migration: complete, to southern states, Mexico and Central America

Food: insects, berries, rarely comes to suet feeders

Compare: The Common Yellowthroat (pg. 289) has a yellow breast, unlike the Yellow-rumped's patches of yellow. The male Yellow Warbler (pg. 293) is all yellow with orange streaks on breast. Male Wilson's Warbler (pg. 285) has a characteristic black crown. Look for a combination of yellow patches on the head, flanks and rump.

Stan's Notes: Common warbler in the state, nesting in conifer and aspen forests on mountains. Formerly called Audubon's Warbler. Sometimes called Butter-butts due to the yellow patch on rump. Males molt to a dull color similar to females each winter, retaining the yellow patches. Most migrate, but in some years many can be found on the coast during winter. Familiar call is a robust "chip."

WESTERN WOOD-PEWEE
Contopus sordidulus

MIGRATION
SUMMER

Size: 6¼" (15.5 cm)

Male: An overall gray bird with darker wings and tail. Two narrow gray wing bars. Dull white throat with pale yellow or white belly. Black upper bill, dull orange lower.

Female: same as male

Juvenile: similar to adult, lacking the two-toned bill

Nest: cup; female builds; 1 brood per year

Eggs: 2-4; pale white with brown markings

Incubation: 12-14 days; female incubates

Fledging: 14-18 days; female and male feed young

Migration: complete, to Central and South America

Food: insects

Compare: An unremarkable bird. Look for the Wood-Pewee's distinctive gray wing bars to help identify.

Stan's Notes: A widespread bird in the state that is most common in aspen forest and near water. It requires trees with dead tops or branches from which to sing and hunt for flying insects, which compose nearly all of the diet. Often returns to the same perch after each foray. Nests throughout western North America from Alaska to Mexico. Overall populations are decreasing about 1 percent each year. Common name comes from a nasal whistle, "pee-wee."

AMERICAN DIPPER
Cinclus mexicanus

YEAR-ROUND

Size: 7½" (19 cm)

Male: Dark gray to black overall, slightly lighter-colored head. Short upturned tail, and dark eyes and bill.

Female: same as male

Juvenile: similar to adult, only paler with white eyelids that are most noticeable when blinking

Nest: pendulous, covered nest with the entrance near the bottom, on cliff, behind waterfall; female builds; 1-2 broods per year

Eggs: 3-5; white without markings

Incubation: 13-17 days; female incubates

Fledging: 18-25 days; female and male feed young

Migration: non-migrator, seeks moving open water

Food: aquatic insects, small fish, crustaceans

Compare: Similar shape as American Robin (pg. 211), but lacks a red breast. The only songbird in the state that dives into fast-moving water.

Stan's Notes: A common bird of fast, usually noisy streams that provide some kind of protected shelf on which to construct nest. Some have had success attracting with man-made ledges. Plunges headfirst into fast-moving water, looking for just about any aquatic insect, propelling itself underwater with wings. Often seen emerging with a large insect, which it smashes against rock before eating. Depending on snowmelt, nesting usually starts in March or April. American Dippers in lower elevations often nest for a second time each season.

MIGRATION
SUMMER

EASTERN KINGBIRD
Tyrannus tyrannus

Size: 8" (20 cm)

Male: Mostly black gray bird with white belly and chin. Black head and tail with a distinctive white band across the end of the tail. Has a concealed red crown that is rarely seen.

Female: same as male

Juvenile: same as adult

Nest: cup; male and female build; 1 brood a year

Eggs: 3-4; white with brown markings

Incubation: 16-18 days; female incubates

Fledging: 16-18 days; female and male feed young

Migration: complete, to Mexico, Central America and South America

Food: insects, fruit

Compare: Rarely confused with other birds. Lacks any yellow of the Western Kingbird (pg. 303). Medium-sized bird, smaller than American Robin (pg. 211). Look for the white band along the end of the tail to identify.

Stan's Notes: A common bird of open fields and prairies. Acting unafraid of other birds and chasing the larger ones, it is perceived as having an attitude. Bold behavior gave rise to its common name, King. Perches on tall branches, watching for insects. After flying out to catch them, it returns to the same perch, a technique called hawking. Male and female return to mating ground and defend a territory together.

gray morph

brown morph

WESTERN SCREECH-OWL
Otus kennicottii

YEAR-ROUND

Size:	8½" (22 cm); up to 1½-foot wingspan
Male:	A small, overall gray owl with bright yellow eyes. Two short ear tufts. A short tail. Some birds are brownish.
Female:	same as male
Juvenile:	similar to adult of the same morph, lacks ear tufts
Nest:	cavity; uses old woodpecker hole; 1 brood per year
Eggs:	2-6; white without markings
Incubation:	21-30 days; female incubates
Fledging:	25-30 days; female and male feed young
Migration:	non-migrator
Food:	insects, small mammals, birds
Compare:	Less than half the size of the Great Horned Owl (pg. 165), it is hard to confuse with its considerably larger cousin.

Stan's Notes: The most common small owl in the western part of the state. An owl of suburban woodland and backyards. Requires trees that are at least a foot in diameter for nesting and roosting, so it usually is found in towns, or in trees that have been preserved. A secondary cavity nester, which means it nests in tree cavities that were created by other birds. Usually not found in elevations above 4,000 feet (1,200 m). Densities in lower elevations are about 1 bird per square mile (up to 3 per sq. km). Most screech-owls are gray; some are brown.

winter

breeding
pg. 115

DUNLIN
Calidris alpina

Size: 8-9" (20-22.5 cm)

MIGRATION
WINTER

Male: Winter adult has a brownish gray back with a light gray chest and white belly. Stout bill curves slightly downward at tip. Black legs.

Female: slightly larger than male, with longer bill

Juvenile: slightly rusty back with spotty chest

Nest: ground; the male and female build; 1 brood per year

Eggs: 2-4; an olive-buff or a blue-green with red-brown markings

Incubation: 21-22 days; male and female incubate, the male during day, female at night

Fledging: 19-21 days; male feeds young, female often leaves before young fledge

Migration: complete, to the coasts of the U.S., Mexico and Central America

Food: insects

Compare: Winter Dunlin has a stout down-turned bill and is overall gray.

Stan's Notes: Usually seen in gray winter plumage from August to early May. Breeding plumage is more commonly seen in spring. Flights include heights up to 100 feet (30 m) with brief gliding alternating with shallow flutters, and rhythmic, repeating song. Huge flocks fly synchronously, with birds twisting and turning, flashing light and dark undersides. The males tend to fly farther south than females in the winter. Doesn't nest in the state.

male

female

AMERICAN ROBIN
Turdus migratorius

Size: 9-11" (22.5-28 cm)

Male: A familiar gray bird with a rusty red breast, and nearly black head and tail. White chin with black streaks. White eye ring.

Female: similar to male, but with a gray head and a duller breast

Juvenile: similar to female, but has a speckled breast and brown back

Nest: cup; female builds with help from the male; 2-3 broods per year

Eggs: 4-7; pale blue without markings

Incubation: 12-14 days; female incubates

Fledging: 14-16 days; female and male feed young

Migration: complete, southern states, Mexico, Central America, non-migrator in Washington

Food: insects, fruit, berries, worms

Compare: Familiar bird to all.

Stan's Notes: Although complete migrators, they can be seen year-round throughout Washington. Why it is that some don't migrate is not known. Can be heard singing all night long in spring. Most people don't realize how easy it is to tell the difference between the male and female robin. Look for the male's dark, nearly black head and brick-red chest, compared with the female's gray head and dull red chest. Robins are not listening for worms when they cock their heads to one side or the other. They are looking with eyes that are placed far back on the sides of their heads. A very territorial bird. Often seen fighting its own reflection in windows.

male

female

YEAR-ROUND

CALIFORNIA QUAIL
Callipepla californica

Size: 10" (25 cm)

Male: Plump gray quail with black face and chin. Prominent teardrop-shaped plume on the forehead. "Scaled" appearance on the belly, light brown to white. Pale brown forehead.

Female: similar to male, lacks a black face and chin

Juvenile: similar to female

Nest: ground; female builds; 1 brood per year

Eggs: 12-16; white with brown markings

Incubation: 18-23 days; female incubates

Fledging: 8-10 days; female and male teach young to feed

Migration: non-migrator

Food: seeds, leaves, insects, visits ground feeders

Compare: Ring-necked Pheasant (pg. 173) is larger and lacks the unique plume on the head of Quail. More common than the Mountain Quail (not shown), which is brown and has an extremely long, thin plume on forehead.

Stan's Notes: A common quail in Washington that has expanded its range in the state over the past 50 years. It prefers open fields, agricultural areas and sagebrush. Not found in dense forest or high elevations. It rarely flies, preferring to run away. Roosts in trees or dense shrubs at night, not on the ground. Usually seen in groups (coveys) of up to 100 individuals during winter, breaking up into small family units for breeding. Young stay with their family group until autumn.

GRAY JAY
Perisoreus canadensis

Size: 11½" (29 cm)

Male: A large gray bird with black nape and white chest. Short black bill and dark eyes. White patch on forehead.

Female: same as male

Juvenile: sooty gray with a faint white whisker mark

Nest: cup; male and female build; 1 brood a year

Eggs: 3-4; gray white, finely marked to unmarked

Incubation: 16-18 days; female incubates

Fledging: 14-15 days; male and female feed young

Migration: non-migrator

Food: insects, seeds, fruit, nuts, visits seed feeders

Compare: Similar size as the Steller's Jay (pg. 63) and Western Scrub-Jay (pg. 65), but lacks the Steller's crest and any blue coloring. Clark's Nutcracker (pg. 217) is slightly larger, with black wings. Black-billed Magpie (pg. 43) is nearly twice as large, with a much longer tail and lacks the white patch on forehead.

Stan's Notes: A bird of conifer woods in middle to high elevations. Called Camp Robber because it rummages through camps looking for scraps of food. Also called Whisky Jack or Canada Jay. Easily tamed, it will fly to your hand if offered raisins or nuts. Will eat just about anything. Also stores extra food for winter, balling it together in a sticky mass, placing it on a tree limb, often concealing it with lichen or bark. Travels in family units of three to five, making good companions for high altitude hikers or climbers. Reminds some of an overgrown chickadee.

215

CLARK'S NUTCRACKER
Nucifraga columbiana

Size: 12" (30 cm)

Male: All-gray bird with black wings and narrow black band down the center of tail. Small white patches on long wings, seen in flight. A relatively short tail with white undertail.

Female: same as male

Juvenile: same as adult

Nest: cup; female and male build; 1 brood a year

Eggs: 2-5; pale green with brown markings

Incubation: 16-18 days; female and male incubate

Fledging: 18-20 days; female and male feed young

Migration: non-migrator

Food: seeds, insects, berries, eggs, mammals

Compare: Slightly larger than the Gray Jay (pg. 215), which lacks the Nutcracker's black wings. The Steller's Jay (pg. 63) is dark blue with a black crest.

Stan's Notes: A high country bird seen in conifer forest in central and eastern parts of the state. Although it has a varied diet, it relies heavily on piñon seeds, often caching large amounts to consume later or feed young. Has a large pouch in throat (sublingual pouch), which it uses to transport seeds. Studies show the birds can carry up to 100 seeds at a time. Nests early in the year while snow still covers the ground, relying on stored foods.

soaring

juvenile

SHARP-SHINNED HAWK
Accipiter striatus

Size: 10-14" (25-36 cm)

Male: Small woodland hawk with gray back and head, and rusty red breast. Long tail with several dark tail bands, widest band at end of squared-off tail. Red eyes.

Female: same as male, only larger

Juvenile: same size as adults, with a brown back and heavily streaked breast, yellow eyes

Nest: platform; female builds; 1 brood per year

Eggs: 4-5; white with brown markings

Incubation: 32-35 days; female incubates

Fledging: 24-27 days; female and male feed young

Migration: complete, southern states, Mexico, Central America, some non-migrators in the state

Food: birds, small mammals

Compare: Nearly identical to Cooper's Hawk (pg. 225), only smaller. Look for squared end of tail on the Sharp-shinned, compared with the round end of Cooper's.

Stan's Notes: A common hawk of backyards and woodland, often seen swooping in on birds visiting feeders. Short rounded wings and long tail allow this hawk to navigate through thick stands of trees in pursuit of prey. Common name comes from the sharp keel on the leading edge of its "shin," although it is actually below rather than above the bird's ankle on the tarsus bone of foot. The tarsus in most birds is round. In flight, head doesn't protrude as far as the head of the Cooper's Hawk.

ROCK DOVE
Columba livia

Size: 13" (33 cm)

Male: No set color pattern. Gray to white, patches of iridescent greens and blues, usually with a light rump patch.

Female: same as male

Juvenile: same as adult

Nest: platform; female builds; 3-4 broods a year

Eggs: 1-2; white without markings

Incubation: 18-20 days; female and male incubate

Fledging: 25-26 days; female and male feed young

Migration: non-migrator

Food: seeds

Compare: The larger Band-tailed Pigeon (pg. 223) is uniformly colored and patterned, and has a disproportionately long tail. Rock Dove is larger than the light brown Mourning Dove (pg. 131).

Stan's Notes: Also known as Domestic Pigeon, it was introduced to North America from Europe by the early settlers. Most common around cities and barnyards, where it scratches for seeds. The wide color variation comes from the years of selective breeding while in captivity. Parents feed young a regurgitated liquid called crop-milk for the first few days of life. One of the few birds that can drink without tilting its head back. Nests beneath bridges, on buildings, balconies, barns and sheds. Once poisoned as a "nuisance city bird," many cities have Peregrine Falcons (not shown) that feed on Rock Doves, keeping their numbers in check.

221

BAND-TAILED PIGEON
Columba fasciata

Size: 14½" (37 cm)

Male: A typical pigeon-shaped body. Overall gray with a narrow white band on nape of neck. Dark eyes. Black-tipped yellow bill. Yellow legs. Disproportionately long tail.

Female: same as male

Juvenile: similar to adult, lacks white band on neck

Nest: cup; the female and male build; 2-3 broods per year

Eggs: 1-2; white without markings

Incubation: 18-20 days; female and male incubate

Fledging: 25-27 days; female and male feed young

Migration: non-migrator

Food: nuts, seeds, fruit, berries

Compare: The smaller Rock Dove (pg. 221) comes in a wide variety of colors and patterns, unlike the uniformly colored and patterned Band-tailed. Look for the long tail, and uniform color of Band-taileds in a flock.

Stan's Notes: A common pigeon in the western half of the state. Prefers residential areas and city parks with suitable large conifer trees, in low to middle elevations. Nomadic lifestyle, moving about constantly in response to the food supply. Often seen in flight. Male performs a courtship flight of a rapid flapping flight that alternates with short glides, then lands and bows to female. Nests in scattered pairs. Easily distinguished from the Rock Dove by its uniform gray color and long tail.

soaring

juvenile

YEAR-ROUND

COOPER'S HAWK
Accipiter cooperii

Size: 14-20" (36-50 cm)

Male: A medium hawk with short wings and a long rounded tail with several black bands. Rusty breast and dark wing tips. Slate gray back. Bright yellow spot at base of gray bill (cere). Red eyes.

Female: similar to male, only slightly larger

Juvenile: brown back with brown streaks on breast, yellow eyes

Nest: platform; male and female build; 1 brood per year

Eggs: 2-4; greenish with brown markings

Incubation: 32-36 days; female and male incubate

Fledging: 28-32 days; male and female feed young

Migration: non-migrator to partial migrator, southern states and Mexico

Food: small birds, mammals

Compare: Nearly identical to the Sharp-shinned Hawk (pg. 219), only larger, darker gray and with a rounded-off tail.

Stan's Notes: A common hawk of the woodland. In flight, look for its large head, short wings and long tail. Short stubby wings help it maneuver between trees while pursuing small birds. Will come to feeders, hunting for unaware birds. Flies with long glides followed by a few quick flaps. Known to ambush prey, it will fly into heavy brush or even run on the ground in pursuit. Nestlings have gray eyes that become bright yellow at 1 year of age and later, dark red.

female pg. 155

male

GADWALL
Anas strepera

Size: 20" (50 cm)

Male: A plump gray duck with a brown head and a distinctive black rump. White belly and chestnut-tinged wings. Bright white wing linings. Small white wing patch, seen when swimming. Gray bill.

Female: similar to female Mallard, a mottled brown with a pronounced color change from dark brown body to light brown neck and head, bright white wing linings, small white wing patch, gray bill with orange sides

Juvenile: similar to female

Nest: ground; lined with fine grass, and down feathers plucked from mother's breast; 1 brood per year

Eggs: 8-11; white without markings

Incubation: 24-27 days; female incubates

Fledging: 48-56 days; young feed themselves

Migration: complete, southern states, central Mexico, non-migrator in Washington

Food: aquatic insects

Compare: Male Gadwall is one of the few gray-colored ducks. Look for its distinctive black rump.

Stan's Notes: A duck of shallow marshes with lots of vegetation. Found in freshwater wetlands in eastern Washington, but is most common in the urban and suburban areas of western Washington, especially in southern parts of Puget Sound. Nests on land within 300 feet (100 m) of water. Establishes pair bond during winter.

male

female pg. 169

NORTHERN HARRIER
Circus cyaneus

Size: 24" (60 cm)

Male: A slim, low-flying hawk. Silver gray with a large white rump patch and a white belly. Faint narrow bands across the tail. Tips of wings black.

Female: dark brown back, a brown-streaked breast and belly, large white rump patch, narrow black bands across tail, tips of wings black

Juvenile: similar to female, with an orange breast

Nest: platform; female and male build; 1 brood per year

Eggs: 4-8; bluish white without markings

Incubation: 31-32 days; female incubates

Fledging: 30-35 days; male and female feed young

Migration: partial to non-migrator, to western coastal U.S., southern states, Mexico and Central America

Food: mice, snakes

Compare: Slimmer than Red-tailed Hawk (pg. 159). Look for black bands on tail and a white rump patch.

Stan's Notes: One of the easiest hawks to identify. Harriers glide just above the ground, following the contours of the land while searching for prey. Wings are held just above the horizontal position, tilting back and forth in the wind, similar to Turkey Vultures. Was formerly called Marsh Hawk due to its habit of hunting over marshes. Nests on the ground. At all ages, the Northern Harrier has distinctive owl-like face disks.

CANADA GOOSE
Branta canadensis

YEAR-ROUND
SUMMER

Size: 25-43" (63-109 cm)

Male: Large gray goose with black neck and head, with a white chin or cheek strap.

Female: same as male

Juvenile: same as adult

Nest: platform; female builds; 1 brood per year

Eggs: 5-10; white without markings

Incubation: 25-30 days; female incubates

Fledging: 42-55 days; male and female teach young to feed

Migration: non-migrator to partial migrator, will move to any place with open water

Food: aquatic plants, insects, seeds

Compare: Large goose that is rarely confused with any other bird.

Stan's Notes: Common year-round residents that have adapted to our changed environment very well and now breed throughout the state. Adults will mate for many years, but only start to breed in their third year. Males often act as sentinels, standing on the edge of the group and bobbing their heads up and down, becoming very aggressive to anybody who approaches. Will hiss as if displaying displeasure. Adults molt their primary flight feathers while raising young, rendering family groups flightless at the same time. Several subspecies vary geographically around the U.S. Generally they are darker in color in the western groups and paler in the eastern. Size decreases northward, with the smallest subspecies found on the Arctic tundra.

SANDHILL CRANE
Grus canadensis

MIGRATION
SUMMER

Size: 40-48" (102-120 cm); up to 7-foot wingspan

Male: Elegant gray bird with long legs and neck. Wings and body often stained rusty brown. Scarlet red cap. Red eyes.

Female: same as male

Juvenile: dull brown, lacks red cap, has yellow eyes

Nest: platform, on the ground; female and male build; 1 brood per year

Eggs: 2; olive with brown markings

Incubation: 28-32 days; female and male incubate

Fledging: 65 days; female and male feed young

Migration: complete, to southern states and Mexico

Food: insects, fruit, worms, plants, amphibians

Compare: Similar size as Great Blue Heron (pg. 235), but Crane has a shorter bill and a red patch on head. The Great Blue Heron flies with its neck held in an S shape, unlike the Crane's straight neck.

Stan's Notes: Among the tallest birds in the world and capable of flying at great heights. Usually seen in large undisturbed fields near water. Often heard before seen, they have a very distinctive rattling call. Plumage often appears rust brown because of staining from mud during preening. Characteristic flight with upstroke quicker than down. For their spectacular mating dance the performers face each other, bow and jump into the air while uttering loud cackling sounds and flapping wings. Frequently flips sticks and grass into the air during dance.

GREAT BLUE HERON
Ardea herodias

YEAR-ROUND
SUMMER

Size: 42-52" (107-132 cm)

Male: Tall gray heron. Black eyebrows extend into several long plumes off the back of head. Long yellow bill. Feathers at base of neck drop down in a kind of necklace.

Female: same as male

Juvenile: same as adult, but more brown than gray, with a black crown and no plumes

Nest: platform; male and female build; 1 brood per year

Eggs: 3-5; blue green without markings

Incubation: 27-28 days; female and male incubate

Fledging: 56-60 days; male and female feed young

Migration: complete, southern states, Mexico, Central America, South America, partial migrator, to western Washington

Food: small fish, frogs, insects, snakes

Compare: Similar size as the Sandhill Crane (pg. 233), but lacks the Crane's red crown. Crane flies with neck held straight, unlike the Heron's S-shaped neck.

Stan's Notes: One of the most common herons, often barking like a dog when startled. Seen stalking small fish in shallow water. Will strike at mice, squirrels and just about anything else it might come across. Flies holding neck in an S shape, with its long legs trailing straight out behind. The wings are held in cupped fashion during flight. Nests in colonies of up to 100 birds. Nests in treetops near or over open water.

235

male

female

CALLIOPE HUMMINGBIRD
Stellula calliope

Size: 3¼" (8 cm)

Male: Iridescent green head, back and tail. Breast and belly white to tan. Iridescent rosy-red throat patch (gorget), V-shaped. Compared with other hummingbirds, has a very short, thin bill and short tail.

Female: same as male, but thin, spotty throat patch

Juvenile: similar to female

Nest: cup; female builds; 1 brood per year

Eggs: 1-2; white without markings

Incubation: 15-17 days; female incubates

Fledging: 18-22 days; female feeds young

Migration: complete, to Central and South America

Food: nectar, insects, will come to nectar feeders

Compare: Smaller than other hummingbirds. Look for the short thin bill and short tail, with tips of wings extending past tail. Female is similar to female Anna's Hummingbird (pg. 239) and Rufous Hummingbird (pg. 251), but has a shorter, thinner bill and short tail.

Stan's Notes: Smallest bird in North America. Common in open forest and brushy areas in lower elevations of eastern Washington, with the females often building nests on branches of pine trees. A relatively quiet bird, it will come to nectar feeders. During breeding season, males can be heard zinging around while displaying for the females. Females are difficult to distinguish from the other female hummingbirds. Juvenile males obtain a partial throat patch by the autumn of their first year.

237

male

female

ANNA'S HUMMINGBIRD
Calypte anna

YEAR-ROUND

Size: 4" (10 cm)

Male: Iridescent green body with dark head, chin and neck. In direct sunlight, the dark head shines a deep rose red. Breast and belly are dull gray. White eye ring.

Female: similar to male, but head reflects only a few red flecks instead of a complete rose red

Juvenile: similar to female

Nest: cup; female builds; 2-3 broods per year

Eggs: 1-3; white without markings

Incubation: 14-19 days; female incubates

Fledging: 18-23 days; female feeds young

Migration: partial to non-migrator, many move to the coast of southern California and Mexico

Food: nectar, insects, will come to nectar feeders

Compare: Slightly larger than Rufous Hummingbird (pg. 251), lacking the characteristic burnt-orange color of the Rufous.

Stan's Notes: Common western coastal hummingbird found from Baja, California, to British Columbia. Unknown in the state before the late 1950s, it has since expanded northward. Now considered common along the coast. Early nesting, with females building tiny cup nests on chaparral-covered hillsides and in canyons. Feathers on the head are black until viewed in direct sun. Reflected sunlight turns the male's head bright rosy red.

male

female

VIOLET-GREEN SWALLOW
Tachycineta thalassina

Size: 5¼" (13.5 cm)

Male: Dull emerald green crown, nape and back. Violet blue wings and tail. White chest and belly. White cheeks with white extending above the eyes. Wings extend beyond the tail when perching.

Female: same as male, only duller

Juvenile: similar to adult of the same sex

Nest: cavity; the female and male build; 1 brood per year

Eggs: 4-6; pale white with brown markings

Incubation: 13-14 days; female incubates

Fledging: 18-24 days; female and male feed young

Migration: complete, to Central and South America

Food: insects

Compare: Similar size as the Cliff Swallow (pg. 89), which has a distinctive tan-to-rust pattern on the head. Barn Swallow (pg. 61) has a distinctive, deeply forked tail. Tree Swallow (pg. 53) is mostly a deep blue, lacking any emerald green of the Violet-green Swallow.

Stan's Notes: Commonly seen throughout Washington. A solitary nester in tree cavities, but rarely underneath cliff overhangs, unlike colony-nesting Cliff Swallows. Like Tree Swallows, can be attracted with nest boxes. Will search for miles for errant feathers to line its nest. Short tail with wing tips extending beyond the end of the tail when perching. Returns to the state in late April. Begins nesting in May. Young often leave the nest by June.

male

female pg. 149

WOOD DUCK
Aix sponsa

Size: 17-20" (43-50 cm)

Male: A small, highly ornamented dabbling duck with a green head and crest patterned with white and black. A rusty chest, white belly and red eyes.

Female: brown, similar size and shape as male, has bright white eye ring and a not-so-obvious crest, blue patch on wing often hidden

Juvenile: same as female

Nest: cavity; female lines old woodpecker cavity; 1 brood per year

Eggs: 10-15; creamy white without markings

Incubation: 28-36 days; female incubates

Fledging: 56-68 days; female teaches young to feed

Migration: complete, to southern states, partial to non-migrator in Washington

Food: aquatic insects, plants, seeds

Compare: Smaller than the male Northern Shoveler (pg. 245) and lacks the long wide bill. Male Green-winged Teal (pg. 137) is less colorful.

Stan's Notes: A common duck of quiet, shallow backwater ponds. Nests in old woodpecker holes or in nest boxes. Often seen flying deep in forest or perched high on tree branches. Female takes flight with loud squealing call and enters nest cavity from full flight. Will lay eggs in a neighboring female nest (egg dumping), resulting in some clutches in excess of 20 eggs. Young stay in nest cavity only 24 hours after hatching, then jump from up to 30 feet (9 m) to the ground or water to follow their mother, never returning to the nest.

male

female pg. 153

NORTHERN SHOVELER
Anas clypeata

YEAR-ROUND
SUMMER

Size: 20" (50 cm)

Male: Medium-sized duck with iridescent green head, rusty sides and white breast. Has an extraordinarily large spoon-shaped bill that is almost always held pointed toward water.

Female: same spoon-shaped bill, brown and black all over and blue wing patch

Juvenile: same as female

Nest: ground; female builds; 1 brood per year

Eggs: 9-12; olive without markings

Incubation: 22-25 days; female incubates

Fledging: 30-60 days; female leads young to food

Migration: complete, southern states, Mexico, Central America, non-migrator in Washington

Food: aquatic insects, plants

Compare: Similar to the male Mallard (pg. 249), but Shoveler has a large, characteristic spoon-shaped bill. Larger than male Wood Duck (pg. 243) and lacks the Wood Duck's crest. Shares the cinnamon-colored sides of male Cinnamon Teal (pg. 141), but is larger.

Stan's Notes: One of several species of shoveler, so called because of the peculiarly shaped bill. The Northern Shoveler is the only species of these ducks in North America. Seen in small flocks of five to ten, swimming low in water with large bills always pointed toward the water, as if they're too heavy to lift. Feeds primarily by filtering tiny plants and insects from the water's surface with bill.

female pg. 267

male

COMMON MERGANSER
Mergus merganser

YEAR-ROUND

Size: 27" (69 cm)

Male: Long, thin, duck-like bird with green head, a black back, and white sides, breast and neck. Has a long, pointed orange bill. Often appears to be black and white in poor light.

Female: same size and shape as the male, but with a rust red head, ragged "hair" on head, gray body with white chest and chin, and long, pointed orange bill

Juvenile: same as female

Nest: cavity; female lines old woodpecker cavity; 1 brood per year

Eggs: 9-11; ivory without markings

Incubation: 28-33 days; female incubates

Fledging: 70-80 days; female feeds young

Migration: partial to non-migrator in Washington

Food: small fish, aquatic insects

Compare: Similar size as male Mallard (pg. 249), but male Common Merganser has a black back, bright white sides and a long pointed bill.

Stan's Notes: Can be found on just about any open water in the winter, but more common along rivers than lakes. Mergansers are shallow water divers that feed on fish in no more than 10 to 15 feet (3 to 4.5 m) of water. The bill has a fine serrated-like edge to help catch slippery fish. Females often lay eggs in other merganser nests (egg dumping), resulting in broods of up to 15 young per mother. The male leaves the female as soon as she starts to incubate eggs. Orphans are accepted by other merganser mothers with young.

female pg. 171

male

MALLARD
Anas platyrhynchos

YEAR-ROUND

Size: 27-28" (69-71 cm)

Male: Large, bulbous green head, white necklace and rust brown or chestnut-colored chest. A combination of gray and white on sides. Yellow bill, legs and feet.

Female: all brown with orange and black bill, small blue and white wing mark (speculum)

Juvenile: same as female, but with a yellow bill

Nest: ground; female builds; 1 brood per year

Eggs: 7-10; greenish to whitish, unmarked

Incubation: 26-30 days; female incubates

Fledging: 42-52 days; female leads young to food

Migration: partial to non-migrator in Washington

Food: seeds, plants, aquatic insects, will come to ground feeders offering corn

Compare: The male Northern Shoveler (pg. 245) has a white chest with rust on sides and a dark spoon-shaped bill. Male Gadwall (pg. 227) lacks the male Mallard's green head.

Stan's Notes: A familiar duck of lakes and ponds. Will return to place of birth. The name "Mallard" comes from the Latin *masculus*, meaning "male," referring to the habit of males not taking part in raising ducklings. Both male and female have white tails and white underwings. Black central tail feathers of male curl upward.

male

female

RUFOUS HUMMINGBIRD
Selasphorus rufus

Size: 3¾" (9.5 cm)

Male: Tiny burnt-orange bird with a black throat patch (gorget) that reflects orange-red in sunlight. White chest. Green-to-tan flanks.

Female: same as male, but lacking the throat patch

Juvenile: similar to female

Nest: cup; female builds; 1-2 broods per year

Eggs: 1-3; white without markings

Incubation: 14-17 days; female incubates

Fledging: 21-26 days; female feeds young

Migration: complete, to Central and South America

Food: nectar, insects, will come to nectar feeders

Compare: Unique bird that is identified by the orange (rufous) coloring.

Stan's Notes: One of the smallest birds in the state. A bold, hardy hummer, often seen well out of its normal range, showing up all along the East coast. Will visit hummingbird feeders in your yard. Doesn't sing, but will chatter or buzz to communicate. Weighing just 2 to 3 gm, it takes about five average-sized hummingbirds to equal the weight of a single chickadee. Heart pumps an incredible 1,260 beats per minute. Male performs a spectacular pendulum-like flight over the perched female. After mating, the female flies off to build a nest and raise young, without any help from her mate. Constructs a soft flexible nest that expands to accommodate the growing young.

female pg. 299

male

BULLOCK'S ORIOLE
Icterus bullockii

Size: 8" (20 cm)

Male: Bright orange and black bird. Black crown, eye line, nape, chin, wings and back with orange elsewhere. Bold white patch on the wings.

Female: dull yellow overall, pale white belly, white wing bars on gray-to-black wings

Juvenile: similar to female

Nest: pendulous; female and male build; 1 brood per year

Eggs: 4-6; pale white to gray, brown markings

Incubation: 12-14 days; female incubates

Fledging: 12-14 days; female and male feed young

Migration: complete, to Central and South America

Food: insects, berries, nectar, visits nectar feeders

Compare: The only oriole that comes to Washington regularly. Look for the male's bright orange and black markings.

Stan's Notes: So closely related to Baltimore Orioles of the eastern U.S., at one time both were considered a single species. Interbreeds with the Baltimore where ranges overlap. Most common in eastern Washington, where cottonwood trees grow along rivers and other wetlands. Also found at edges of clearings, in city parks, on farms and along irrigation ditches. Hanging sock-like nest is constructed of plant fibers such as the inner bark of junipers and willows. Will incorporate yarn and thread into its nest if offered at the time of nest building.

female pg. 113

male

BLACK-HEADED GROSBEAK
Pheucticus melanocephalus

Size: 8" (20 cm)

Male: Stocky bird with burnt orange chest, neck and rump. Black head, tail and wings with irregular-shaped white wing patches. Large bill with upper bill darker than lower.

Female: appears like an overgrown sparrow, overall brown with lighter-colored chest and belly, bold white eyebrows, large two-toned bill

Juvenile: similar to adult of the same sex

Nest: cup; female builds; 1 brood per year

Eggs: 3-4; pale green or bluish, brown markings

Incubation: 11-13 days; female and male incubate

Fledging: 11-13 days; female and male feed young

Migration: complete, to Mexico, Central America and South America

Food: insects, seeds, fruit

Compare: Same size as the male Evening Grosbeak (pg. 301), but male Black-headed has an orange breast and lacks a yellow belly. Look for its large bicolored bill.

Stan's Notes: A cosmopolitan bird that nests in a wide variety of habitats, seeming to prefer the foothills in the western part of the state slightly more than other places. Both males and females sing, and aggressively defend their nests against intruders. Song is very similar to the American Robin's and Western Tanager's, making it difficult to tell them apart by song. Populations are increasing in Washington and across the U.S.

male

female

VARIED THRUSH
Ixoreus naevius

Size: 9½" (24 cm)

Male: Potbellied robin-like bird with orange eyebrows, chin, breast and wing bars. Head, neck and back are gray to blue. Black breast band and eye mark.

Female: browner version of male, lacking the black breast band

Juvenile: similar to female

Nest: cup; female builds; 1-2 broods per year

Eggs: 3-5; pale blue with brown markings

Incubation: 12-14 days; female incubates

Fledging: 10-15 days; female and male feed young

Migration: partial migrator to non-migrator, to West coast states

Food: insects, fruit

Compare: Similar size and shape as American Robin (pg. 211), but has a warm-orange breast, compared with the brick-red breast of the Robin. Male Varied Thrush has a distinctive black breast band.

Stan's Notes: An intriguing-looking bird. Nests in Alaska, Canada and mountains in Washington and Oregon. Prefers moist conifer forest. Most common in dense, older conifer forests in high elevations. Moves to lower elevations during the winter where it is often seen in towns and orchards and thickets, or migrates to California. Seen in flocks during winter of up to 20 birds. Well known for individual birds to fly eastward in winter, showing up in just about any state, then returning to the West coast for breeding.

257

yellow male

female pg. 77

male

HOUSE FINCH
Carpodacus mexicanus

YEAR-ROUND

Size: 5" (13 cm)

Male: An orange red face, breast and rump, with a brown cap. Brown marking behind eyes. Brown wings streaked with white. A white belly with brown streaks.

Female: brown with heavily streaked white chest

Juvenile: similar to female

Nest: cup, sometimes in cavities; female builds; 2 broods per year

Eggs: 4-5; pale blue, lightly marked

Incubation: 12-14 days; female incubates

Fledging: 15-19 days; female and male feed young

Migration: non-migrator to partial migrator, will move around to find food

Food: seeds, fruit, leaf buds, will visit seed feeders

Compare: Male Cassin's Finch (pg. 263) is similar, but is a rosy red, unlike the orange red of male House Finch, and lacks a brown cap. Look for the streaked chest and belly, and brown cap of male House Finch.

Stan's Notes: Very social bird. Visits feeders in small flocks. Likes nesting in hanging flower baskets. Incubating female fed by male. Loud, cheerful warbling song. Suffers a fatal eye disease that causes eyes to crust over. Historically it occurred from the Pacific coast to the Rocky Mountains, with a few reaching the eastern side. Birds introduced to Long Island, New York, in the 1940s have populated the entire eastern U.S. Now found all over the U.S. Rarely, some males are yellow (see inset) instead of red, probably due to poor diet.

259

female pg. 93

male

PURPLE FINCH
Carpodacus purpureus

YEAR-ROUND
WINTER

Size: 6" (15 cm)

Male: Raspberry-red head, cap, breast, back and rump. Brownish wings and tail.

Female: heavily streaked brown and white bird with large white eyebrows

Juvenile: same as female

Nest: cup; female and male build; 1 brood a year

Eggs: 4-5; greenish blue with brown markings

Incubation: 12-13 days; female incubates

Fledging: 13-14 days; female and male feed young

Migration: irruptive, moves around in search of food

Food: seeds, insects, fruit, comes to seed feeders

Compare: Redder than the orange red of male House Finch (pg. 259), with a clear (no streaking) red breast. The male House Finch has a brown cap, compared with the male Purple Finch's red cap. Similar to the male Red Crossbill (pg. 265), but lacks the unique long crossed bill.

Stan's Notes: A year-round resident, common in non-residential areas. Preferring open woods or woodland edges of low to middle elevation conifer forest, it has been replaced in cities by the House Finch. Feeds primarily on seeds, with the seeds of ash trees a very important food source. Will come to seed feeders along with House Finches, making it hard to tell them apart. A rich loud song, with a distinctive "tic" note made only in flight. Travels in flocks of up to 50. Nests in May. Not a purple color, the Latin name *purpureus* means "crimson" or other reddish color.

male

female pg. 95

YEAR-ROUND
WINTER

CASSIN'S FINCH
Carpodacus cassinii

Size: 6½" (16 cm)

Male: Overall light wash of crimson red with an especially bright red crown. Distinct brown streaks on back and wings. White belly.

Female: overall brown to gray, fine black streaks on the back and wings, heavily streaked white chest and belly

Juvenile: similar to female

Nest: cup; female builds; 1-2 broods per year

Eggs: 3-5; white without markings

Incubation: 12-14 days; female incubates

Fledging: 14-18 days; female and male feed young

Migration: partial migrator to non-migrator, will move around to find food

Food: seeds, insects, fruits, berries, will visit seed feeders

Compare: Similar to the male House Finch (pg. 259), which has a brown cap, is heavily streaked on flanks and is orange red, unlike the male Cassin's rosy red.

Stan's Notes: A common mountain finch of eastern Washington's conifer forests. Usually forages for seeds on the ground, but also eats evergreen buds, and aspen and willow catkins. Breeds in May. Colony nester, depending on the regional food source. The more food available, the larger the colony. Male sings a fast warble, often imitating other birds such as jays, tanagers and grosbeaks. Even though it is a cowbird host, its population has increased over the past 20 years.

female pg. 295

male

RED CROSSBILL
Loxia curvirostra

Size: 6½" (16 cm)

Male: A dirty-red-to-orange sparrow-sized bird. Bright red crown and rump. Long, pointed, crossed bill. Dark brown wings and tail. Short tail.

Female: pale yellow chest, light-gray throat patch, a crossed bill, dark brown wings and tail

Juvenile: streaked with tinges of yellow, bill gradually crosses about two weeks after fledging

Nest: cup; female builds; 1 brood per year

Eggs: 3-4; bluish white with brown markings

Incubation: 14-18 days; female incubates

Fledging: 16-20 days; female and male feed young

Migration: non-migrator to irruptive, moves around the state in winter to find food

Food: seeds, leaf buds, comes to seed feeders

Compare: Similar in shape, size and color to the male Purple Finch (pg. 261). Look for the male Red Crossbill's unique bill.

Stan's Notes: The long crossed bill is adapted for extracting seeds from pine and spruce cones, its favorite food. Often dangles upside down like a parrot to reach cones. Also seen on the ground where it eats grit, which helps digest food. Plumage can be highly variable among individuals. Nests in conifer forest at any elevation, mainly west of the Cascades. Although a resident nester, migrating crossbills from farther north move to the state during winter, searching for food, swelling populations. This irruptive behavior makes them more common during some winters and scarce in others.

male pg. 247

female

COMMON MERGANSER
Mergus merganser

YEAR-ROUND

Size: 27" (69 cm)

Female: A long, thin, duck-like bird with a rust red head and ragged "hair" on the back of head. Gray body with white chest and chin. Long, pointed orange bill.

Male: same size and shape as the female, but with a green head, black back, white sides and chest, and long, pointed orange bill

Juvenile: same as female

Nest: cavity; female lines old woodpecker cavity; 1 brood per year

Eggs: 9-11; ivory without markings

Incubation: 28-33 days; female incubates

Fledging: 70-80 days; female feeds young

Migration: partial to non-migrator in Washington

Food: small fish, aquatic insects

Compare: Hard to confuse with other birds. Look for ragged "hair" on back of a red head, a long, pointed orange bill, white chest and chin.

Stan's Notes: Can be found on just about any open water in the winter, but more common along rivers than lakes. Mergansers are shallow water divers that feed on fish in no more than 10 to 15 feet (3 to 4.5 m) of water. The bill has a fine serrated-like edge to help catch slippery fish. Females often lay eggs in other merganser nests (egg dumping), resulting in broods of up to 15 young per mother. The male leaves the female as soon as she starts to incubate eggs. Young that lose their mothers will be accepted by other merganser mothers with young.

breeding

winter

in flight

WINTER

MEW GULL
Larus canus

Size: 16" (40 cm)

Male: White gull with dark gray back and wings. Black wing tips. Red ring around dark eyes. Yellow legs. Breeding has a small unmarked yellow bill. Winter plumage has a brown-streaked head and neck, with a dark ring around the tip of yellow bill.

Female: same as male

Juvenile: gray to brown overall with a black-tipped yellow bill

Nest: ground; the female and male build; 1 brood per year

Eggs: 2-3; brown with brown markings

Incubation: 24-26 days; female and male incubate

Fledging: 30-32 days; female and male feed young

Migration: complete, western coastal U.S. and Mexico

Food: insects, fish, shellfish, fruit

Compare: Much smaller than Herring Gull (pg. 277) and Glaucous-winged Gull (pg. 279). Look for the tiny yellow bill and diminutive size.

Stan's Notes: Small gull with a remarkably small bill. A common winter visitor, often seen with other gulls. Often drops sea urchins from heights to crack open and eat. A three-year gull, taking three years to reach maturity. Starts out entirely light brown. Second year resembles the non-breeding adult, with brown-streaked head and neck. Third year has breeding plumage. Doesn't nest in the state, nesting in northwestern Canada and Alaska instead. Young return to natal colony to nest. Known in Europe as Common Gull.

winter

juvenile

breeding

RING-BILLED GULL
Larus delawarensis

Size: 19" (48 cm)

Male: A white bird with gray wings, black wing tips spotted with white, and a white tail, as seen in flight. Yellow bill with a black ring near tip. Yellowish legs and feet. Winter or non-breeding adult has a speckled brown back of head and nape of neck.

Female: same as male

Juvenile: mostly gray version of adult, has dark band at end of tail

Nest: ground; the female and male build; 1 brood per year

Eggs: 2-4; off-white with brown markings

Incubation: 20-21 days; female and male incubate

Fledging: 20-40 days; female and male feed young

Migration: partial migrator to complete, along western coastal U.S., to southern states and Mexico

Food: insects, fish, scavenges

Compare: Smaller than the California Gull (pg. 273), which has a larger bill with a red and black mark near the tip, and dark eyes, compared with the Ring-billed's light-colored eyes.

Stan's Notes: A common gull of garbage dumps and parking lots. Nests in eastern Washington, sometimes nesting in mixed colonies with other gull species. Defends small area around nest, usually a few feet. Spends winters on the coast. A three-year gull with a new, different plumage in each of the first three autumns. Attains ring on bill after the first winter. Attains adult plumage the third year.

winter

breeding

MIGRATION
SUMMER
WINTER

CALIFORNIA GULL
Larus californicus

Size: 21" (53 cm)

Male: White bird with gray wings and black wing tips. A red and black mark on tip of yellow bill. Red ring around dark eyes. Winter or non-breeding adult has brown streaks on back of head and nape of neck.

Female: same as male

Juvenile: all brown for the first two years, similar to adult by third year

Nest: ground; the female and male build; 1 brood per year

Eggs: 2-5; pale brown or olive, brown markings

Incubation: 24-26 days; female and male incubate

Fledging: 40-45 days; female and male feed young

Migration: partial migrator to complete, along western coastal U.S. and Mexico

Food: insects, seeds, mammals

Compare: Larger than the Ring-billed Gull (pg. 271), which lacks California Gull's dark eyes and red mark on bill.

Stan's Notes: Famed gull species that saved the Mormons from the great grasshopper plague in 1848 and inspired gull monuments in Salt Lake City. A four-year gull, the first two years appearing nearly all brown. Third year is similar to the winter adult. Usually doesn't nest until the fourth year, when it obtains adult plumage. Nests in large colonies in southeastern Washington, with up to 1,000 nests. Moves to the coast for the winter. Named for its usual winter sites along the California coast.

winter

in flight

breeding

CASPIAN TERN
Sterna caspia

Size: 21" (53 cm)

Male: White chest and belly. White wing surfaces below and light gray above, with black tips, as seen in flight. Light gray back. Black cap extends over eyes. Large dark red bill with darker tip. Black legs. Winter plumage has a streaked cap.

Female: same as male

Juvenile: similar to winter adult, orange bill

Nest: ground; the female and male build; 1 brood per year

Eggs: 1-4; pinkish with brown markings

Incubation: 20-22 days; female and male incubate

Fledging: 30-40 days; female and male feed young

Migration: complete, to coastal Mexico

Food: fish, aquatic insects

Compare: Smaller and more streamlined than most gulls, with thinner wings than gull wings. Look for the large red bill and black cap.

Stan's Notes: The largest and strongest of our terns. Gives a deep, harsh loud scream. Has been expanding in western Washington over the past 20 years. Often seen in large groups flying at about 30 feet (9 m) above water, patrolling for fish. Nests in large colonies on small islands and sand beaches. The young recognize the calls of their parents, which helps them locate each other when adults return to the colony with food. Young chase after adults until they are fed. Adults feed young for up to seven months, the longest time of any tern species.

breeding

winter

HERRING GULL
Larus argentatus

MIGRATION
WINTER

Size: 23-26" (58-66 cm)

Male: Snow-white bird with slate gray wings and black wing tips with tiny white spots. Bill is yellow with an orange-red spot near tip of the lower bill. Pinkish legs. Winter plumage head and neck are dirty gray to brown.

Female: same as male

Juvenile: uniformly mottled brown to gray, black bill

Nest: ground; the female and male build; 1 brood per year

Eggs: 2-3; olive with brown markings

Incubation: 24-28 days; female and male incubate

Fledging: 35-36 days; female and male feed young

Migration: complete, to coasts that remain unfrozen in North America

Food: fish, insects, clams, eggs, baby birds

Compare: Larger than the Ring-billed Gull (pg. 271), which has yellowish legs and a black ring around its bill, and lacks an orange-red dot on the lower mandible.

Stan's Notes: Common gull of large lakes. An opportunistic bird, scavenging for food from dumpsters, but will also take other birds' eggs and young right from nest. Often drops clams and other shellfish from heights to break shells and get to the soft interior. Nests in colonies, returning to same site year after year. Lines ground nest with grasses and seaweed. Takes about four years for juveniles to obtain adult plumage. Adults molt to a dirty gray in the winter, and look similar to juveniles.

winter

in flight

breeding

GLAUCOUS-WINGED GULL
Larus glaucescens

YEAR-ROUND
WINTER

Size: 26" (66 cm)

Male: White gull with light gray back and wings. Yellow bill with red spot on the lower bill. Dark eyes. Pink legs. Winter plumage has a brown-streaked head and neck.

Female: same as male

Juvenile: gray to brown overall with a black bill

Nest: ground; the female and male build; 1 brood per year

Eggs: 1-3; olive with brown markings

Incubation: 27-29 days; female and male incubate

Fledging: 35-55 days; female and male feed young

Migration: complete to partial migrator, along western coastal U.S. and Mexico

Food: insects, fish, shellfish, garbage

Compare: Herring Gull (pg. 277) is similar in size and color, but Glaucous-winged Gull has gray-tipped wings, unlike the black wing tips of Herring Gull.

Stan's Notes: A four-year gull, taking four years to reach maturity. Starts out entirely gray to brown. Second year is a light gray with patches of white. Third year has a brown-streaked head and neck, but with a gray back, gray wings and a white body, resembles the non-breeding adult. Fourth year is breeding plumage. Returns to same nesting colony each year, often breeding with mate from the previous year. Male bends forward and pops head up while calling for mate.

blue morph

white morph

MIGRATION

SNOW GOOSE
Chen caerulescens

Size: 25-38" (63-96 cm)

Male: A mostly white goose with varying patches of black and brown. Black wing tips. Pink bill and legs. Some birds are grayish with a white head.

Female: same as male

Juvenile: overall dull gray with dark bill

Nest: ground; female builds; 1 brood per year

Eggs: 3-5; white without markings

Incubation: 23-25 days; female incubates

Fledging: 45-49 days; female and male teach young to feed

Migration: complete, to New Mexico and California, southern states and Mexico

Food: aquatic insects and plants

Compare: Smaller than the Canada Goose (pg. 231), lacking a black neck and white chin strap.

Stan's Notes: Two color morphs. The more common white morph is pure white with black wing tips. Gray morph is often called blue, with a white head, gray chest and back, and pink bill and legs. Has a thick serrated bill for pulling up plants. Breeds in large colonies on the tundra of northern Canada. Females don't breed until they are 2 to 3 years old. Older females produce more eggs and are more successful than the younger females. Seen by the thousands during spring and fall migrations.

GREAT EGRET
Ardea alba

Size: 38" (96 cm)

Male: Tall, thin, elegant all-white bird with long, pointed yellow bill. Black stilt-like legs and black feet.

Female: same as male

Juvenile: same as adult

Nest: platform; male and female build; 1 brood per year

Eggs: 2-3; light blue without markings

Incubation: 23-26 days; female and male incubate

Fledging: 43-49 days; female and male feed young

Migration: complete, to southern states, Mexico and Central America

Food: fish, aquatic insects, frogs, crayfish

Compare: Smaller in size and similar in shape to Great Blue Heron (pg. 235), but the Great Egret is all white with black legs and a yellow bill.

Stan's Notes: A tall and stately bird, the Great Egret slowly stalks shallow wetlands looking for small fish to spear with its long sharp bill. Nests in colonies of up to 100 birds. Now protected, they were hunted to near extinction in the 1800s and early 1900s for their long white plumage. The name "Egret" came from the French word *aigrette*, which means "ornamental tufts of plumes." The plumes are grown near the tail during breeding season.

female

male

WILSON'S WARBLER
Wilsonia pusilla

Size: 4¾" (12 cm)

Male: Dull yellow upper and bright yellow lower. Distinctive black cap. Large black eyes and small thin bill.

Female: same as male, but lacking the black cap

Juvenile: similar to female

Nest: cup; female builds; 1 brood per year

Eggs: 4-6; white with brown markings

Incubation: 10-13 days; female incubates

Fledging: 8-11 days; female and male feed young

Migration: complete, to coastal Texas, Central America and Mexico

Food: insects

Compare: Yellow Warbler (pg. 293) is brighter yellow with orange streaking on the male's chest. Male American Goldfinch (pg. 287) has a black forehead and black wings. Common Yellowthroat (pg. 289) has a very distinctive black mask.

Stan's Notes: A widespread warbler of low to mid-level elevations west of the Cascades. Can be found near water in willow and alder thickets. All-insect diet makes it one of the top insect-eating birds in the state. Frequently flicks tail and spreads wings when hopping among thick shrubs, looking for insects. Females often mate with males that have the best territories and that might already have mates (polygyny).

male

winter male

female

AMERICAN GOLDFINCH
Carduelis tristis

YEAR-ROUND
WINTER

Size: 5" (13 cm)

Male: A perky yellow bird with a black patch on forehead. Black tail with conspicuous white rump. Black wings with white wing bars. No marking on the chest. Dramatic change in color during winter, similar to female.

Female: dull olive yellow without a black forehead, with brown black wings and white rump

Juvenile: same as female

Nest: cup; female builds; 1 brood per year

Eggs: 4-6; pale blue without markings

Incubation: 10-12 days; female incubates

Fledging: 11-17 days; female and male feed young

Migration: partial migrator, flocks of up to 20 move around North America

Food: seeds, insects, will come to seed feeders

Compare: The Pine Siskin (pg. 75) and female House Finch (pg. 77) have streaked breasts. Male Yellow Warbler (pg. 293) is all yellow with orange streaks on the chest. Male Wilson's Warbler (pg. 285) lacks black wings.

Stan's Notes: Most often found in open fields, scrubby areas and in woodland. Often called Wild Canary. A feeder bird that enjoys Nyger Thistle. Late summer nesting, uses the silky down from wild thistle for nest. Appears roller-coaster-like in flight. Listen for it to twitter during flight. Almost always in small flocks.

SUMMER

COMMON YELLOWTHROAT
Geothlypis trichas

Size: 5" (13 cm)

Male: Olive brown bird with bright yellow throat and breast, a white belly and a distinctive black mask outlined in white. A long, thin, pointed black bill.

Female: same as male, only lacking black mask

Juvenile: same as female

Nest: cup; female builds; 2 broods per year

Eggs: 3-5; white with brown markings

Incubation: 11-12 days; female incubates

Fledging: 10-11 days; female and male feed young

Migration: complete, to southern states, Mexico and Central America

Food: insects

Compare: Found in a similar habitat as the American Goldfinch (pg. 287), but lacks the male's black forehead and wings. The male Yellow Warbler (pg. 293) has fine orange streaks on chest and lacks the black mask. Yellow-rumped Warbler (pg. 199) has only spots of yellow. Male Wilson's Warbler (pg. 285) lacks the Yellowthroat's black mask.

Stan's Notes: A common warbler of open fields and marshes. Has a cheerful, well-known song, "witchity-witchity-witchity-witchity." The male performs a curious courtship display, bouncing in and out of tall grass while uttering an unusual song. The young remain dependent upon the parents longer than most warblers. A frequent cowbird host.

MIGRATION
SUMMER

ORANGE-CROWNED WARBLER
Vermivora celata

Size: 5" (13 cm)

Male: An overall pale yellow bird with a dark line through eyes. Faint streaking on sides and chest. Small thin bill. Tawny orange crown, often invisible.

Female: same as male, but very slightly duller, often indistinguishable in the field

Juvenile: same as adults

Nest: cup; female builds; 1-2 broods per year

Eggs: 3-6; white with brown markings

Incubation: 12-14 days; female incubates

Fledging: 8-10 days; female and male feed young

Migration: complete, to coastal states, Central America and Mexico

Food: insects, fruit, nectar

Compare: Yellow Warbler (pg. 293) is brighter yellow with orange streaking on the male's chest. Wilson's Warbler (pg. 285) is also brighter yellow with a distinct black cap. Common Yellowthroat (pg. 289) has very distinctive black mask.

Stan's Notes: A widespread bird across the state. Nesting resident, but often seen more during migration. Bulky, well-concealed nests are constructed on the ground with the rim of nest at ground level. Known to feed at sapsucker taps or from flower nectar. The orange crown tends to be hidden and is rarely seen in the field. A widespread breeder, from western Texas to Alaska and across Canada.

male

female

SUMMER

YELLOW WARBLER
Dendroica petechia

Size: 5" (13 cm)

Male: Yellow warbler with orange streaks on the chest and belly. Long, pointed dark bill.

Female: same as male, but lacking orange streaking

Juvenile: similar to female, only much duller

Nest: cup; female builds; 1 brood per year

Eggs: 4-5; white with brown markings

Incubation: 11-12 days; female incubates

Fledging: 10-12 days; female and male feed young

Migration: complete, to southern states, Mexico, and Central and South America

Food: insects

Compare: Look for orange streaking on chest of male. Orange-crowned Warbler (pg. 291) is paler yellow. Male American Goldfinch (pg. 287) has black wings and forehead. The female Yellow Warbler is similar to the female American Goldfinch (pg. 287), but lacks white wing bars. Similar to male Wilson's Warbler (pg. 285), which has a black cap, and lacks orange streaks on chest and belly.

Stan's Notes: A widespread and common warbler in Washington, seen in gardens and shrubby areas near water. Prolific insect eater, gleaning small caterpillars and other insects from tree leaves. Male is often seen higher up in trees than the female bird. Female is less conspicuous. Starts to migrate in August and returns in late April. Males arrive a week or two before the females to claim territories. Migrates at night in mixed flocks of warblers. Rests and feeds days.

female

male pg. 265

RED CROSSBILL
Loxia curvirostra

YEAR-ROUND
WINTER

Size: 6½" (16 cm)

Female: A pale yellow-gray sparrow-sized bird with a pale yellow chest and light gray patch on the throat. Long, pointed, crossed bill. Dark brown wings and tail. Short tail.

Male: dirty-red-to-orange bird, bright red crown and rump, a crossed bill, dark brown wings and tail, short tail

Juvenile: streaked with tinges of yellow, bill gradually crosses about two weeks after fledging

Nest: cup; female builds; 1 brood per year

Eggs: 3-4; bluish white with brown markings

Incubation: 14-18 days; female incubates

Fledging: 16-20 days; female and male feed young

Migration: non-migrator to irruptive, moves around the state in winter to find food

Food: seeds, leaf buds, comes to seed feeders

Compare: Similar in shape and size to female Purple Finch (pg. 93). Look for the female Red Crossbill's unique bill.

Stan's Notes: The long crossed bill is adapted for extracting seeds from pine and spruce cones, its favorite food. Often dangles upside down like a parrot to reach cones. Also seen on the ground where it eats grit, which helps digest food. Plumage can be highly variable among individuals. Nests in conifer forest at any elevation, mainly west of the Cascades. Migrating crossbills from farther north move to the state in winter, searching for food, swelling populations. This makes them more common in some winters and scarce in others.

non-breeding male

breeding male

female

WESTERN TANAGER
Piranga ludoviciana

Size: 7¼" (18.5 cm)

Male: A canary yellow bird with a red head. Black back, tail, wings. One white and one yellow wing bar. Non-breeding lacks the red head.

Female: duller than male, lacking the red head

Juvenile: similar to female

Nest: cup; female builds; 1 brood per year

Eggs: 3-5; light blue with brown markings

Incubation: 11-13 days; female incubates

Fledging: 13-15 days; female and male feed young

Migration: complete, to Mexico and Central America

Food: insects, fruit

Compare: Male American Goldfinch (pg. 287) has a black forehead and lacks the breeding male Tanager's red head. Unique combination of colors makes the male hard to misidentify. Female Bullock's Oriole (pg. 299) lacks the female Tanager's single yellow wing bars.

Stan's Notes: Most common in the western half of the state. The male is stunning in its breeding plumage. Feeds mainly on insects such as bees, wasps, grasshoppers and cicadas. Feeds to a lesser degree on fruit. Male will feed the female as she incubates. Female builds a cup nest in a horizontal fork of a conifer tree, well away from the main trunk, from 20 to 40 feet (6 to 12 m) above ground. The farthest nesting tanager species, reaching far up into Canada's Northwest Territories. An early fall migrant, often seen migrating in late July, with non-breeding males lacking red-colored heads. Can be seen in just about any habitat during migration.

male pg. 253

female

BULLOCK'S ORIOLE
Icterus bullockii

Size:	8" (20 cm)
Female:	Dull yellow head and chest. Gray-to-black wings with white wing bars. A pale white belly. Gray back, as seen in flight.
Male:	bright orange and black, bold white patch on wings
Juvenile:	similar to female
Nest:	pendulous; female and male build; 1 brood per year
Eggs:	4-6; pale white to gray, brown markings
Incubation:	12-14 days; female incubates
Fledging:	12-14 days; female and male feed young
Migration:	complete, to Central and South America
Food:	insects, berries, nectar, visits nectar feeders
Compare:	The only oriole that comes to Washington regularly. Smaller female Western Tanager (pg. 297) has a black back, unlike female Oriole's gray back. Look for the overall dull yellow and gray colors of the female Oriole.

Stan's Notes: So closely related to Baltimore Orioles of the eastern U.S., at one time both were considered a single species. Interbreeds with the Baltimore where ranges overlap. Most common in eastern Washington, where cottonwood trees grow along rivers and other wetlands. Also found at edges of clearings, in city parks, on farms and along irrigation ditches. Hanging sock-like nest is constructed of plant fibers such as the inner bark of junipers and willows. Will incorporate yarn and thread into its nest if offered at the time of nest building.

male

female

EVENING GROSBEAK
Coccothraustes vespertinus

Size: 8" (20 cm)

Male: A striking bird with a stocky body, a large ivory-to-greenish bill and bright yellow eyebrows. Dirty-yellow head, black-and-white wings and tail, and yellow rump and belly.

Female: similar to male, with softer colors, and gray head and throat

Juvenile: same as female, but with a brown bill

Nest: cup; female builds; 1 brood per year

Eggs: 3-4; blue with brown markings

Incubation: 12-14 days; female incubates

Fledging: 13-14 days; female and male feed young

Migration: non-migrator to irruptive, moves around to find food

Food: seeds, insects, fruit, comes to seed feeders

Compare: Larger than its close relative, the American Goldfinch (pg. 287). Look for the dark head with bright yellow eyebrows and the extra-large bill.

Stan's Notes: One of the largest finches. Characteristic undulating finch-like flight. An unusually large bill for cracking seeds, its main food source. Often seen on gravel roads eating gravel, from which it gets minerals, salts and grit to grind the seeds it eats. It is more obvious during winter because it moves in large flocks, searching for food, often coming to feeders. Sheds the outer layer of its bill in spring, exposing a blue green bill.

WESTERN KINGBIRD
Tyrannus verticalis

Size: 9" (22.5 cm)

Male: Bright yellow belly and yellow under wings. Gray head and chest, often with white chin. Wings and tail are dark gray to nearly black with white outer edges on tail.

Female: same as male

Juvenile: similar to adult, less yellow and more gray

Nest: cup; female and male build; 1 brood a year

Eggs: 3-4; white with brown markings

Incubation: 18-20 days; female incubates

Fledging: 16-18 days; female and male feed young

Migration: complete, to Central America

Food: insects, berries

Compare: The Eastern Kingbird (pg. 205) lacks any yellow of the Western Kingbird. Western Meadowlark (pg. 305) shares the Western Kingbird's yellow belly, but has a distinctive black V-shaped necklace.

Stan's Notes: A bird of open country, often seen sitting on top of the same shrub or fence post. Hunts by watching for insects, such as bees, grasshoppers and crickets, then flying out to catch them and returning to its perch. Parents often bring wounded insects back to the nest to have young chase, thus learning how to hunt. Returns in April, nest building in May. Often builds nest in the fork of a small single trunk tree. More common in eastern half of the state, where nearly every stand of trees around a homestead or farm is home to a pair of Western Kingbirds.

WESTERN MEADOWLARK
Sturnella neglecta

Size: 9" (22.5 cm)

Male: Heavy-bodied bird with a short tail. Brown back, lemon-yellow chest and a prominent black V-shaped necklace. White outer tail feathers.

Female: same as male

Juvenile: same as adult

Nest: cup, on the ground in dense cover; female builds; 1-2 broods per year

Eggs: 3-5; white with brown markings

Incubation: 13-15 days; female incubates

Fledging: 11-13 days; female and male feed young

Migration: partial to non-migrator in Washington

Food: insects, seeds

Compare: Western Kingbird (pg. 303) shares a yellow belly, but lacks the Meadowlark's distinctive black V-shaped necklace.

Stan's Notes: Most common in open country in the eastern part of the state. Named "Meadowlark" because it's a bird of meadows and sings like larks of Europe. Best known for its wonderful song. Not a member of the lark family, it belongs to the blackbird family. Related to blackbirds such as Red-wingeds and orioles. Like other members of the blackbird family, the meadowlark catches prey by poking its long thin bill into places such as holes in the ground or in tufts of grass, where insects are hiding. Opening its mouth to create some space, the bird extracts the bugs. Often seen perching on fence posts, it will quickly dive into tall grass when approached. Conspicuous white markings on sides of its very short, stubby tail.

HELPFUL RESOURCES:

Birder's Bug Book, The. Waldbauer, Gilbert. Cambridge: Harvard University Press, 1998.

Birder's Dictionary. Cox, Randall T. Helena, MT: Falcon Press Publishing, 199...

Birder's Handbook, The. Ehrlich, Paul, David S. Dobkin and Darryl Wheye. Ne... York: Simon and Schuster, 1988.

Birds Do It, Too: The Amazing Sex Life of Birds. Harrison, George and Kit Harrison. Minocqua, WI: Willow Creek Press, 1997.

Birds of Forest, Yard, and Thicket. Eastman, John. Mechanicsburg, PA: Stackpol... Books, 1997.

Birds of North America. Kaufman, Kenn. New York: Houghton Mifflin, 2000.

Blackbirds of the Americas. Orians, Gordon. Seattle: University of Washington Press, 1985.

Breeding Birds of Washington State. Smith, Michael R., Philip W. Mattocks, Jr. and Kelly M. Cassidy. Seattle: Seattle Audubon Society, 1997.

Cry of the Sandhill Crane, The. Grooms, Steve. Minocqua, WI: NorthWord Pres... 1992.

Dictionary of American Bird Names, The. Choate, Ernest A. Boston: Harvard Common Press, 1985.

Everything You Never Learned About Birds. Rupp, Rebecca. Pownal, VT: Storey Publishing, 1997.

Field Guide to the Birds of North America, Third Edition. Washington, DC: National Geographic Society, 1999.

Field Guide to Warblers of North America, A. Dunn, Jon and Kimball Garrett. Boston: Houghton Mifflin, 1997.

Field Guide to Western Birds, A. Peterson, Roger Tory. Boston: Houghton Mifflin 1998.

Folklore of Birds. Martin, Laura C. Old Saybrook, CT: Globe Pequot Press, 199...

Guide to Bird Behavior, A: Vol I, II, III. Stokes, Donald and Lillian Stokes. Boston Little, Brown and Company, 1989.

How Birds Migrate. Kerlinger, Paul. Mechanicsburg, PA: Stackpole Books, 1995.

Lives of Birds, The: Birds of the World and Their Behavior. Short, Lester L. Collingdale, PA: DIANE Publishing, 2000.

Living on the Wind. Weidensaul, Scott. New York: North Point Press, 2000.

National Audubon Society: North American Birdfeeder Handbook. Burton, Robert.

York: Dorling Kindersley Publishing, 1995.

onal Audubon Society: The Sibley Guide to Birds. Sibley, David Allen. New
: Alfred A. Knopf, 2000.

ographic Guide to North American Raptors, A. Wheeler, Brian K. and William
lark. New York: Academic Press, 1999.

t Lives of Birds, The. Gingras, Pierre. Toronto: Key Porter Books, 1997.

ts of the Nest. Dunning, Joan. Boston: Houghton Mifflin, 1994.

rows and Buntings: A Guide to the Sparrows and Buntings of North America and
World. Byers, Clive, Jon Curson and Urban Olsson. New York: Houghton
lin, 1995.

es Bluebird Book: The Complete Guide to Attracting Bluebirds. Stokes, Donald
Lillian Stokes. Boston: Little, Brown and Company, 1991.

es Field Guide to Birds: Western Region. Stokes, Donald and Lillian Stokes.
on: Little, Brown and Company, 1996.

es Purple Martin Book. Stokes, Donald and Lillian Stokes. Boston: Little,
vn and Company, 1997.

reporting unusual bird sightings or to hear a recording of where birds
e been seen, contact:

hington Statewide   Southeastern
-454-2662   208-882-6195

er Columbia Basin
-943-6957

EB PAGES:

Internet has become a valuable place to learn about birds. The following are a
web sites that will assist you in your pursuit of birds. You might find birding on
net a fun way to learn more about birds or to spend a long winter night.

E	ADDRESS
shington Ornithological Society	www.wos.org
ional Audubon of Washington	http://wa.audubon.org
erican Birding Association	www.americanbirding.org
nell Lab of Ornithology	www.birds.cornell.edu
hor Stan Tekiela's home page	www.naturesmart.com

ABOUT THE AUTHOR:

Stan Tekiela is a naturalist, author and wildlife photographer with a Bachelor of Science degree in Natural History from the University of Minnesota. He has been a professional naturalist for over 20 years and is a member of the Minnesota Naturalist Association, the Outdoor Writers Association of America and Canon Professional Services. Stan actively studies and photographs birds throughout the U.S. He received an Excellence in Interpretation award from the National Association for Interpretation, and a regional award for Commitment to Outdoor Education. A columnist and radio personality, his syndicated column appears in more than 20 cities and he can be heard on a number of radio stations. Stan resides in Victoria, Minnesota, with wife Katherine and daughter Abigail. He can be contacted via his web page at www.naturesmart.com.

OTHER BOOKS BY STAN TEKIELA:

Birds of Colorado Field Guide
Birds of Iowa Field Guide
Birds of Oregon Field Guide
Trees of Minnesota Field Guide
Wildflowers of Wisconsin Field Guide
Nature Smart: A Family Guide to Nature
Start Mushrooming: The Easiest Way to Collect Edible Mushrooms
And many more titles for additional states